I0502551

Celebrity Caricatures 2013
or
How to draw caricatures of people of note from the past year

Text and illustrations copyright 2013 by Lee P. Sauer
Printed in the United States
ISBN-13: 978-1494739515
ISBN-10: 1494739518

Summary: Step-by-step instructions on how to draw caricatures of people of note in the year 2013. Subjects include Johnny Manziel, Jennifer Lawrence, Miley Cyrus, LeBron James, Prince George, Hillary Clinton, Michelle Obama, Pope Francis, Barack Obama and Nelson Mandela. Start with basic shapes, then add details. Aimed at ages 12 and up. This book is part of the *Drawing From History* series, which teaches both history and drawing.

C&C Press
www.drawingsmiles.com
drawingsmiles@yahoo.com

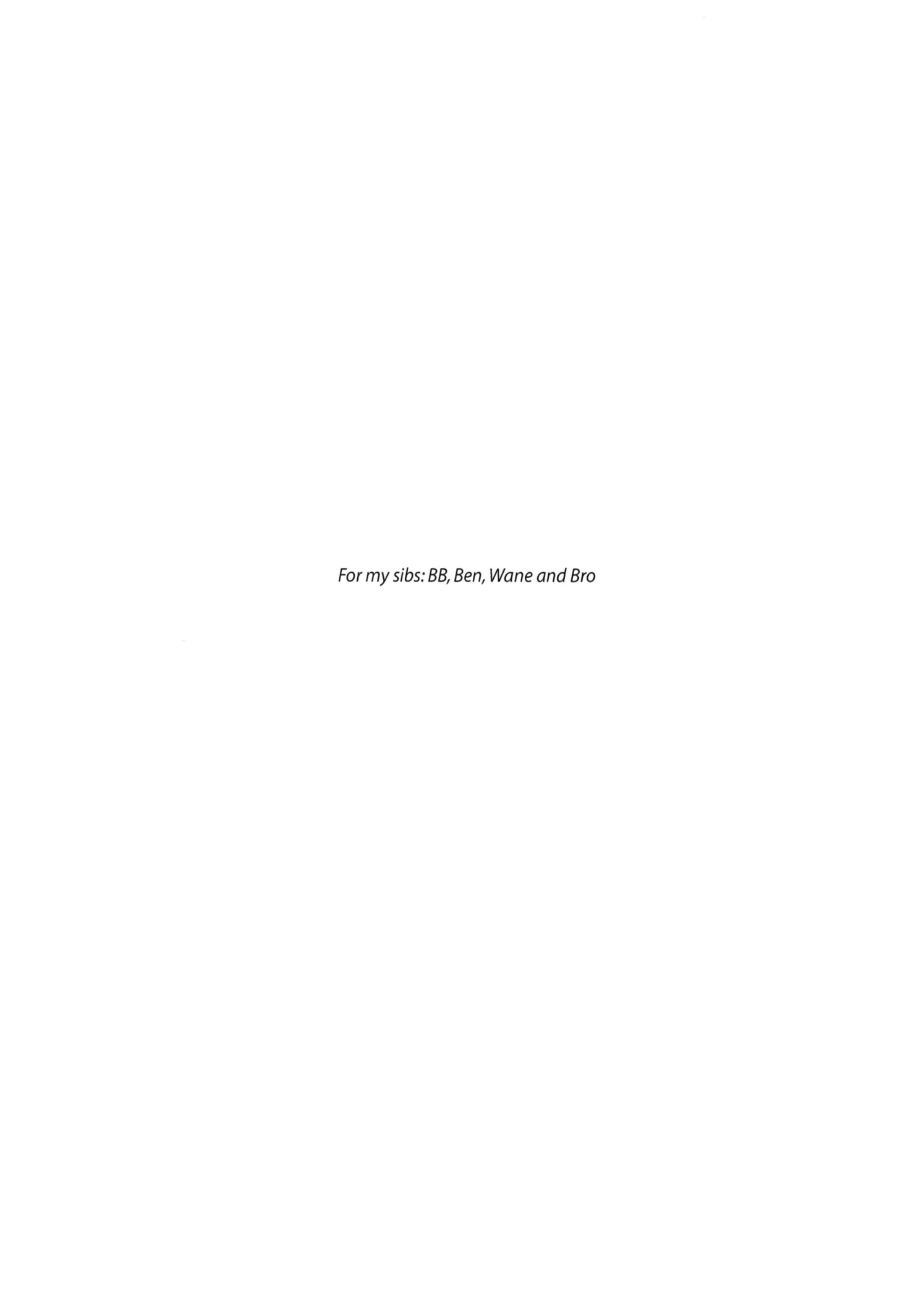

For my sibs: BB, Ben, Wane and Bro

Interested in current events?
Want to learn to draw?
Need illustrations for a school report?
Stuck in prison and bored out of your gourd?
Then this book is for you.

Celebrity Caricatures 2013 has chosen 10 people from the past year as caricature subjects. They may have done great things. Or they may have gotten into trouble. They were chosen for many reasons, but the two most important were:

      1. Did they have an impact?

And, 2. Are they fun to draw?

Enough talk. Get out your pencil and enjoy!

To make the drawings in this book, all you need is a pencil and paper. But, if you want to use real artist equipment, visit **www.drawingfromhistory.com.** There you will find a list of supplies and links to suppliers.

#10
Johnny "Football" Manziel

He won the 2012 Heisman Trophy, given to the best college football player. Then all through 2013, cameras focused on him. Most of the pictures caught Johnny having fun off the field.

Here is a finished caricature of Johnny Football. You can see the steps used to make this drawing on the following pages.

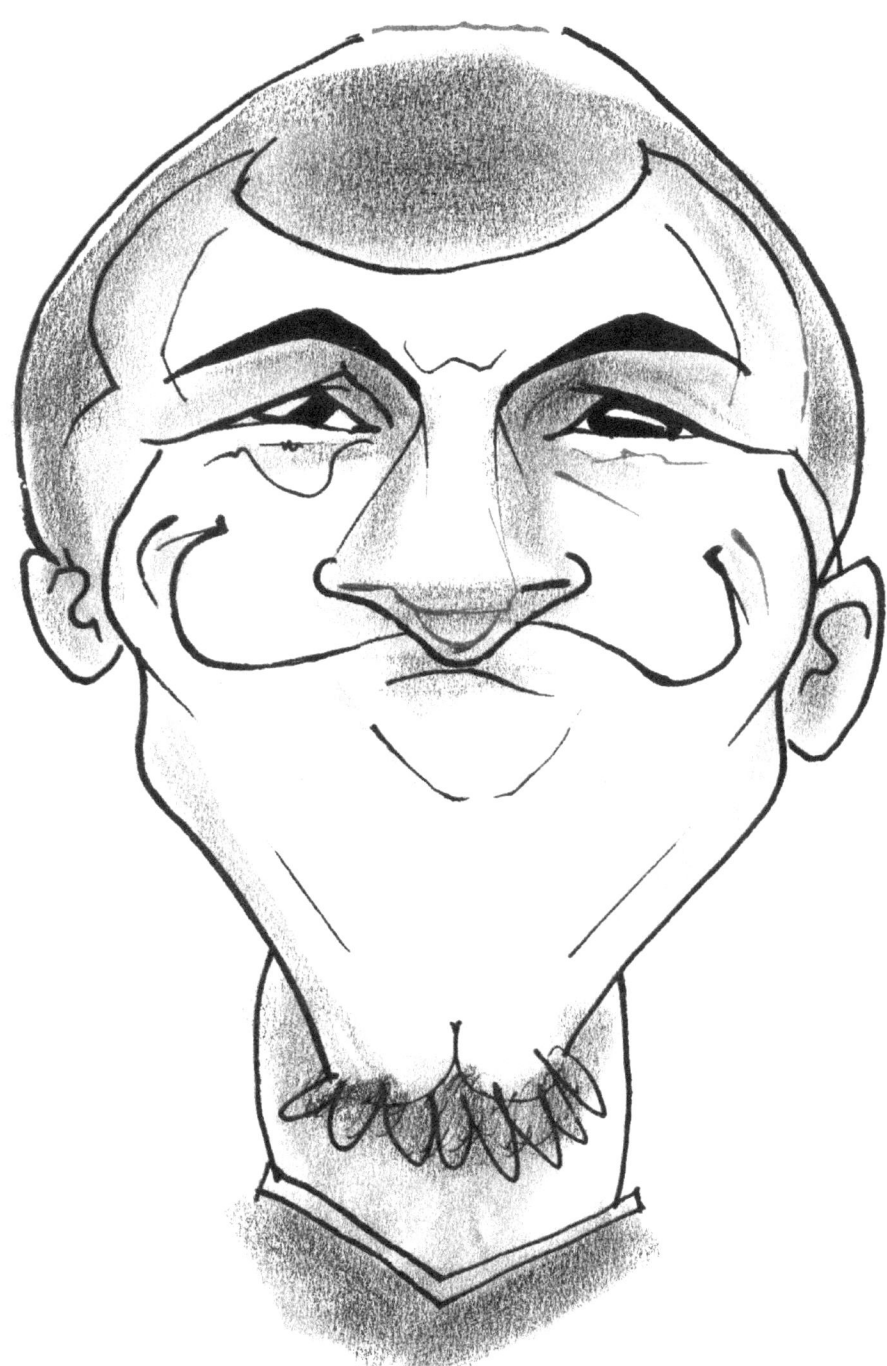

See how to shade!
Go to *www.drawingfromhistory.com* to watch a video on shading.

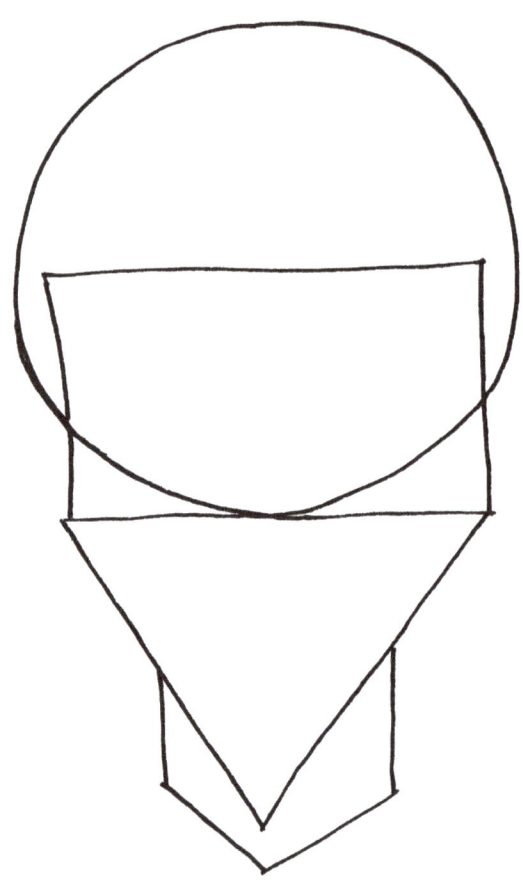

Start each drawing with simple shapes.

Next, add big details . . .

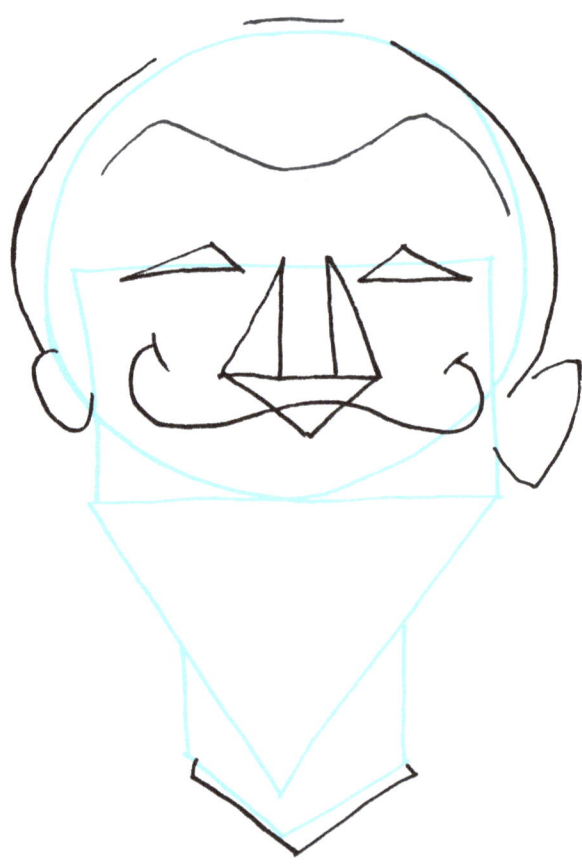

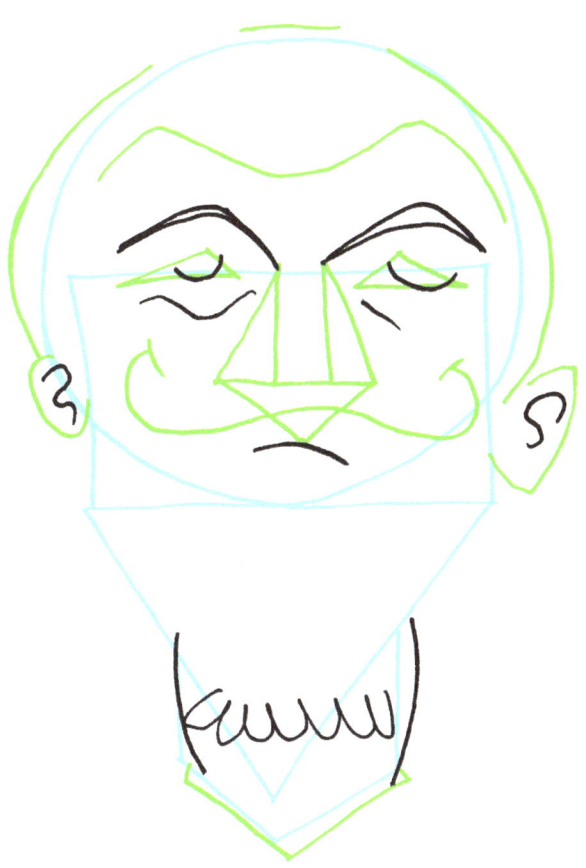

.... **and** small details.

In the final step, round off sharp edges.
Give the drawing life!

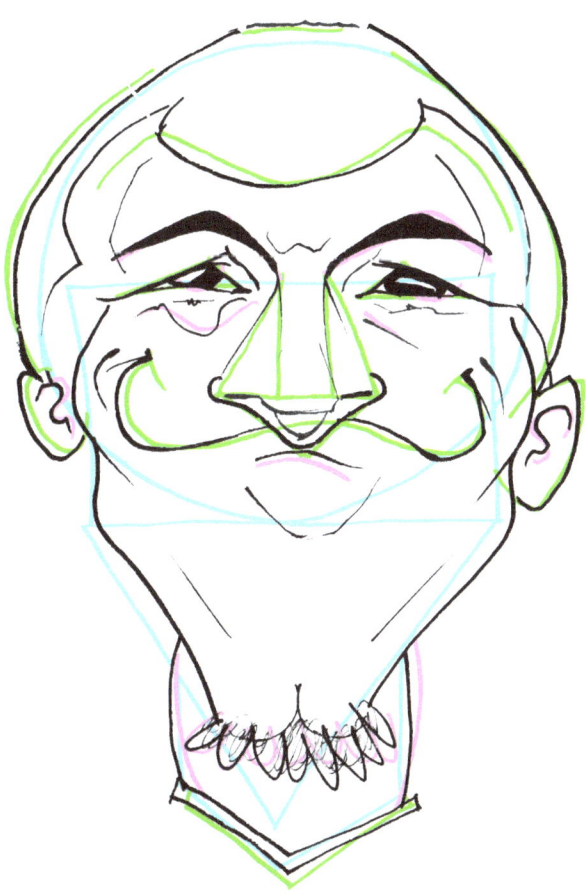

#9
Jennifer Lawrence

She stars in the hit movie series, *Hunger Games*. Too bad she plays the part of a hunted human. When she is not acting, Lawrence shows personality and humor.

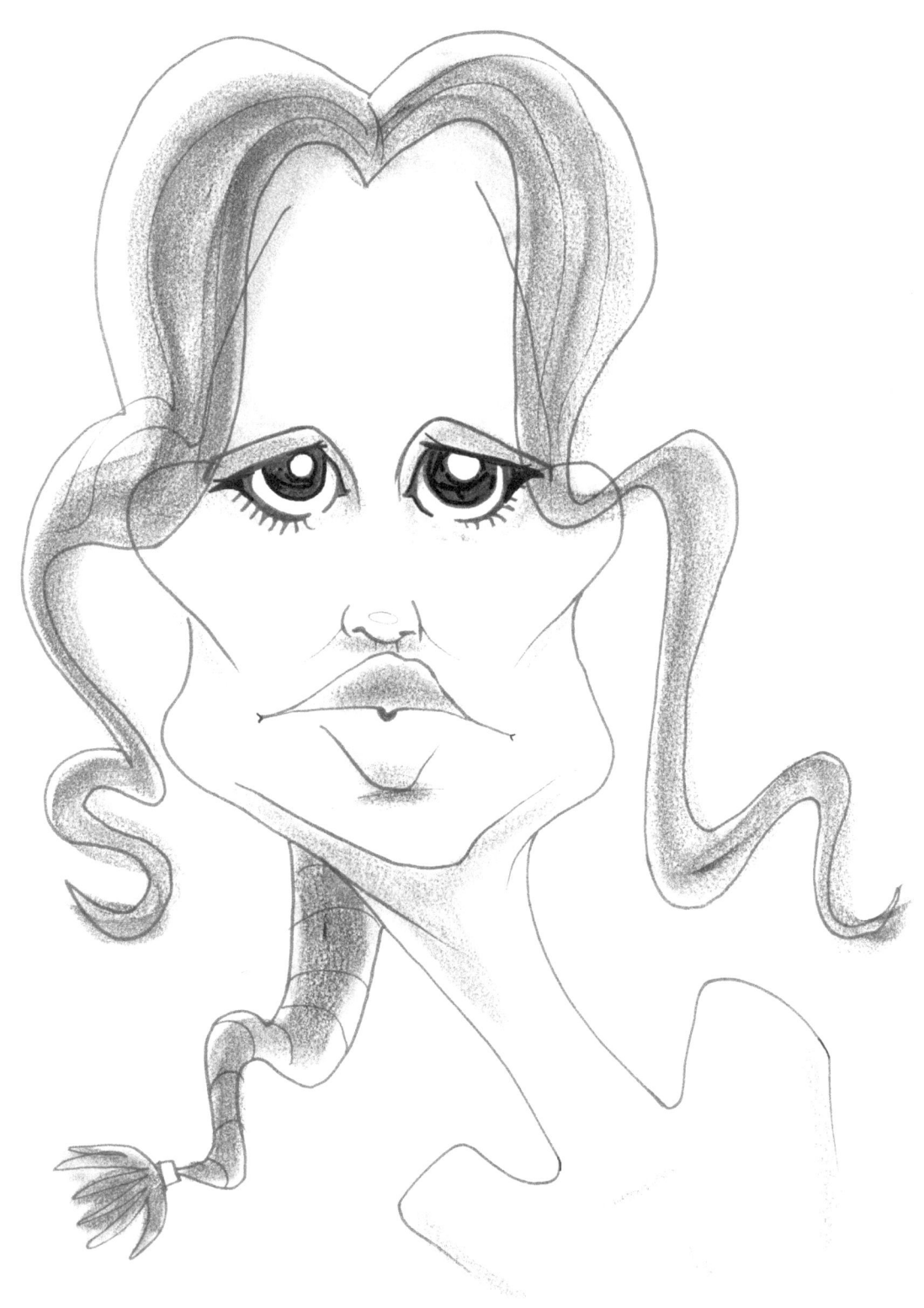

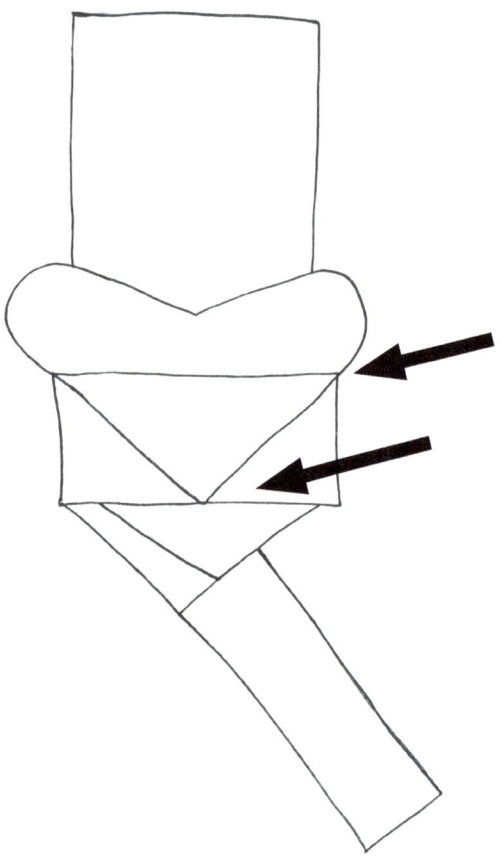

Look for relationships between shapes. For example, the heart shape rests on the bottom of the rectangle. It also leaves the box at the corners on each side.

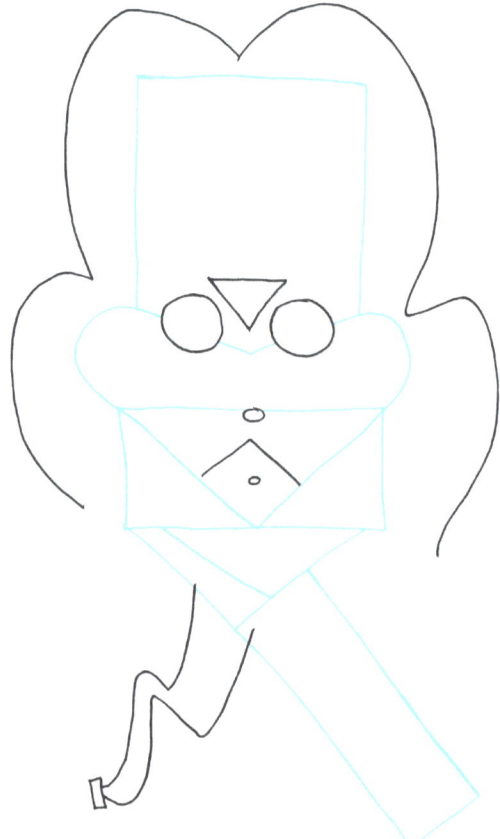

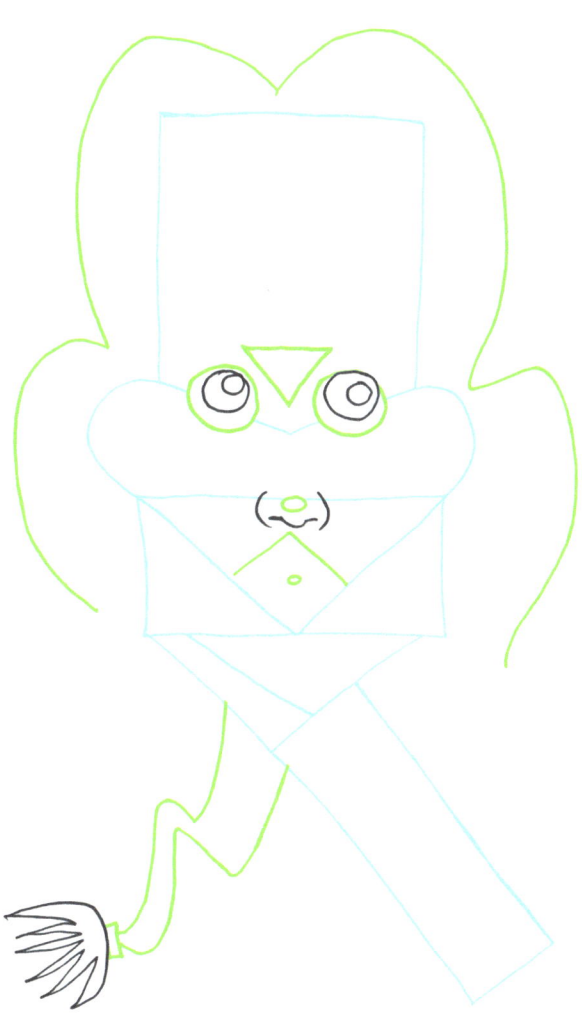

Lines have personality. Sharp turns are abrupt, full of action. Smooth curves are gentle, soft. Thick lines are strong, bold. Thin lines are weak, tender. Match your lines to your subject.

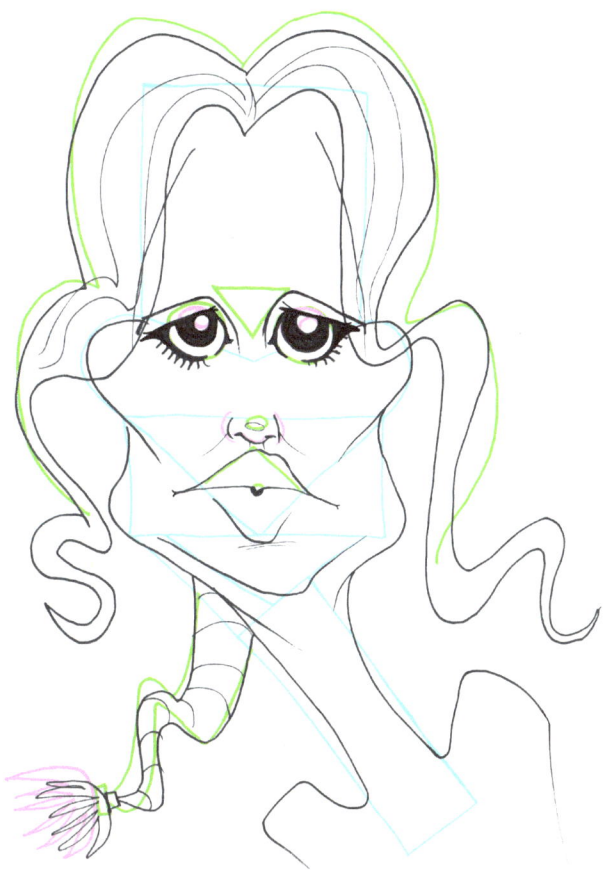

#8
Miley Cyrus

The former child TV star grew up in full view of the world.
And, yes, it is as embarrassing as it sounds.

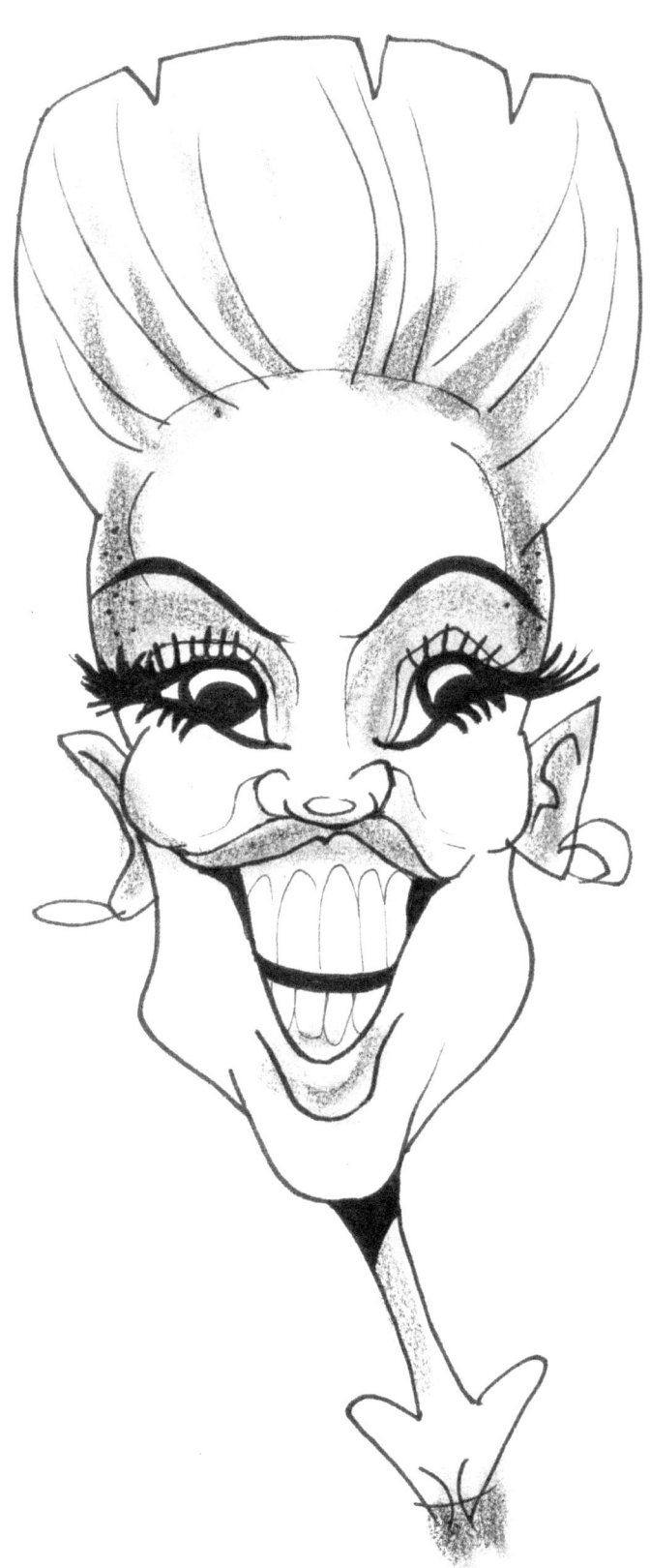

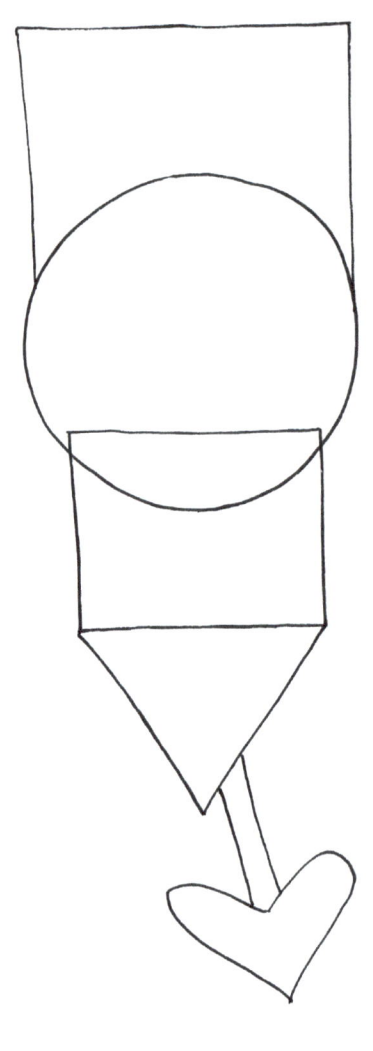
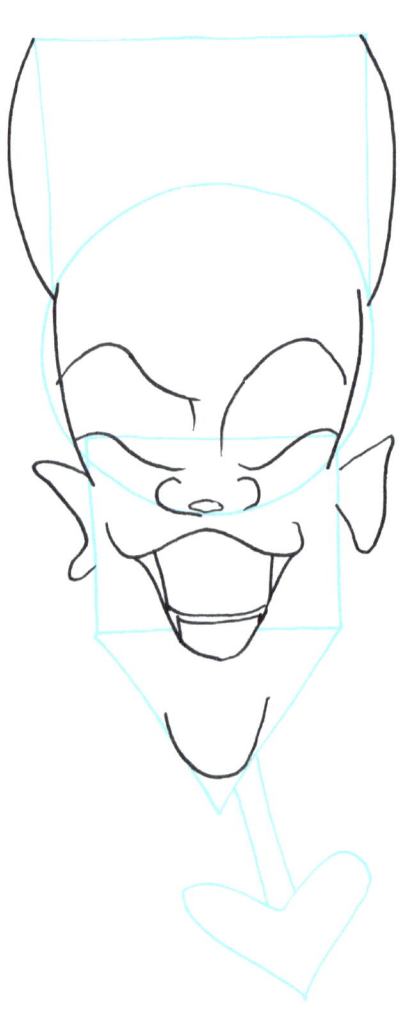

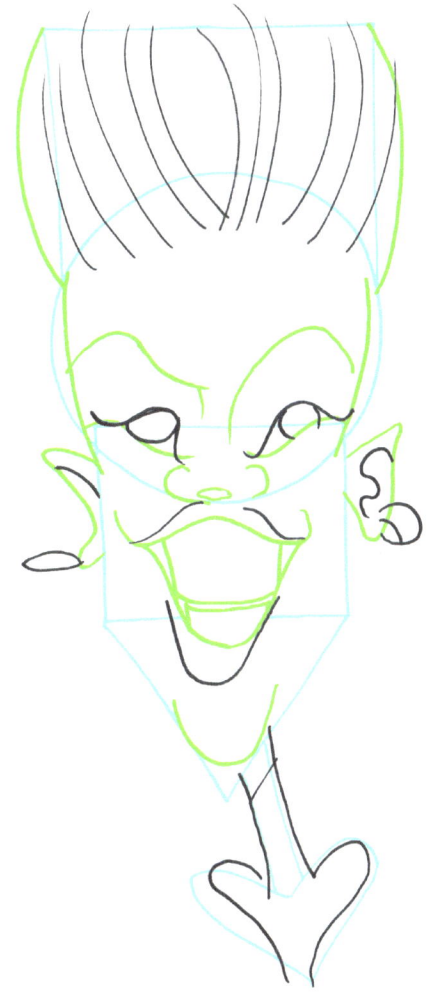

Miley is spunky and brash. Show this with contrast. Look for areas to make solid dark, such as around her eyes and mouth.

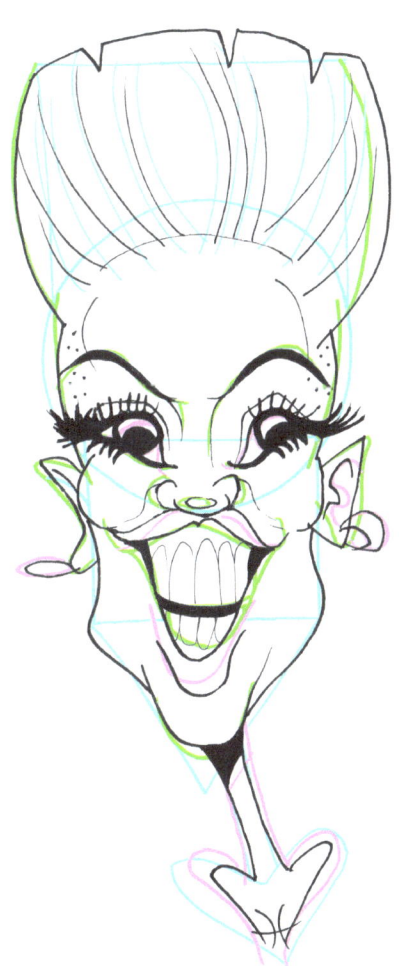

#7

LeBron James

He is considered the best basketball player in the world. As 2013 came to an end, LeBron chased his third NBA championship in a row.

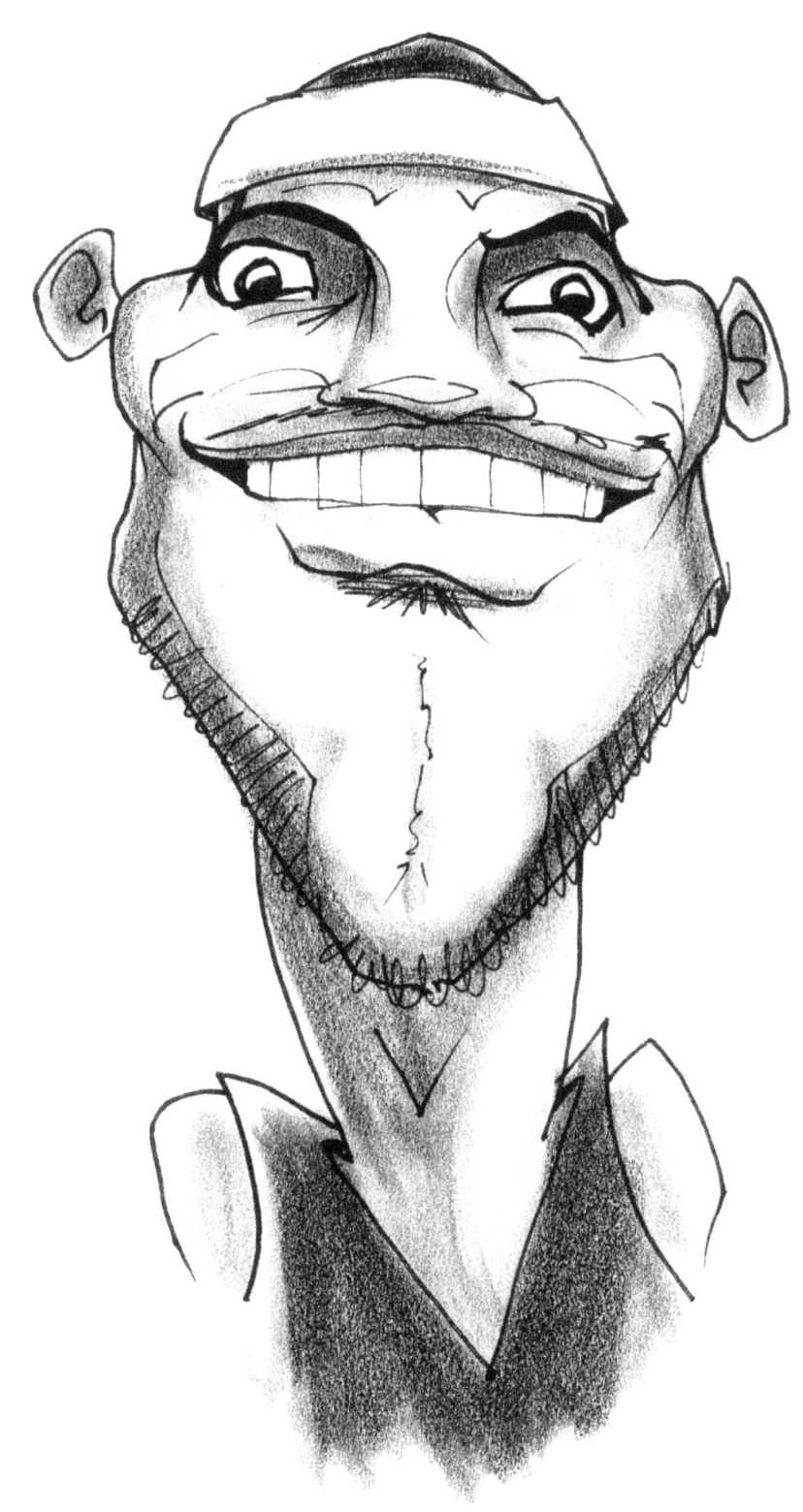

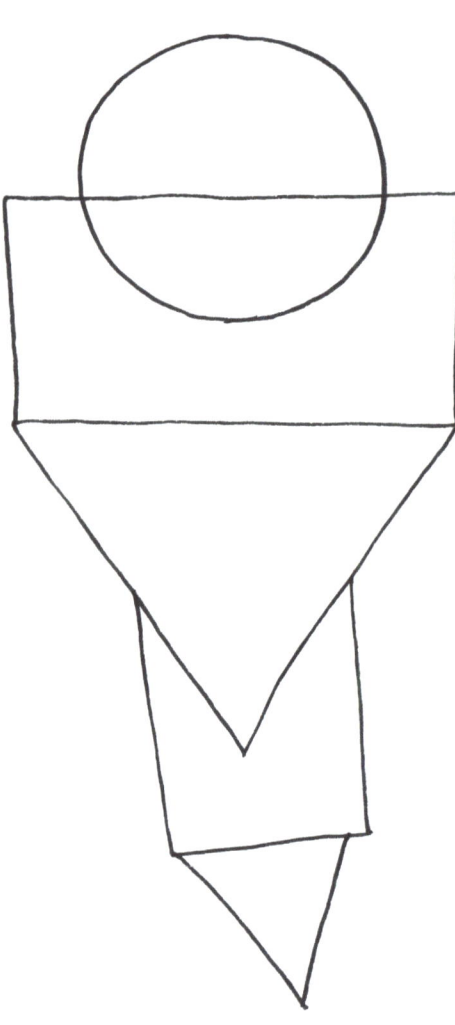

LeBron is known for strength. To show this, emphasize his jaw and chin.

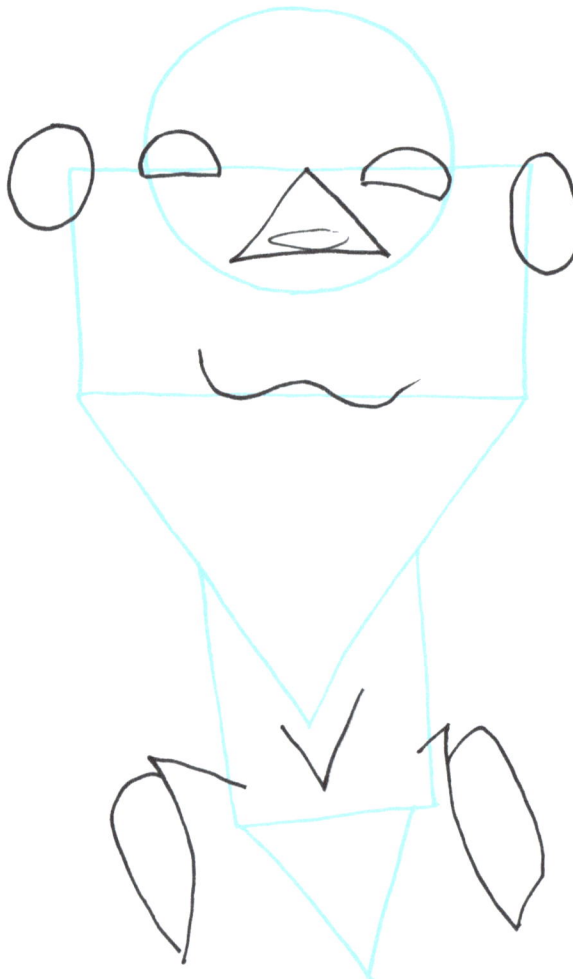

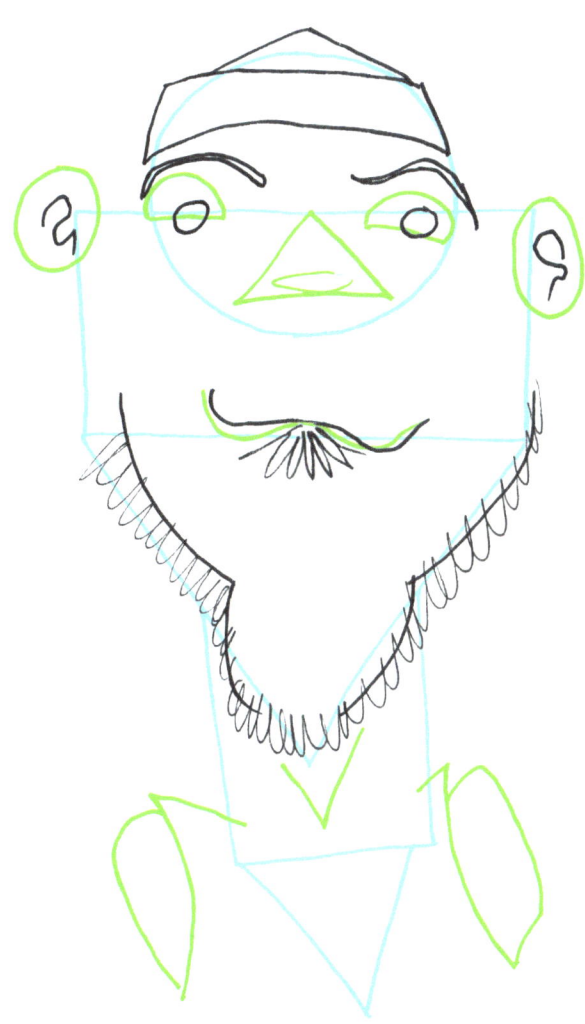
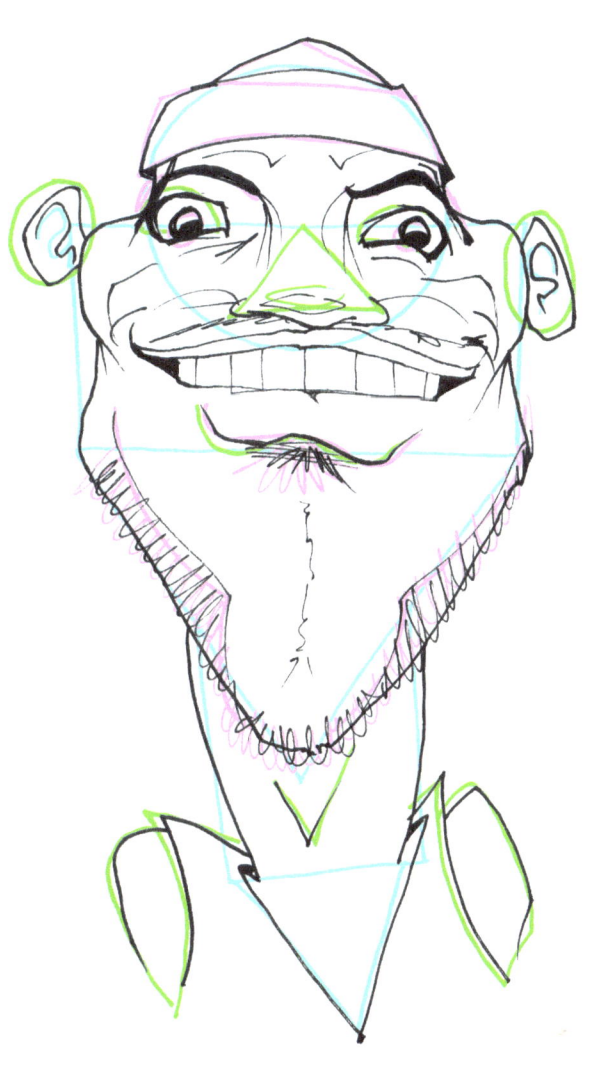

#6

Prince George

Q: What is more fun than a royal wedding?
A: A royal birth

Prince George was born to Britain's Prince William and Kate Middleton in July. If you missed his birth, do not worry. You will hear a lot about the prince in the years to come.

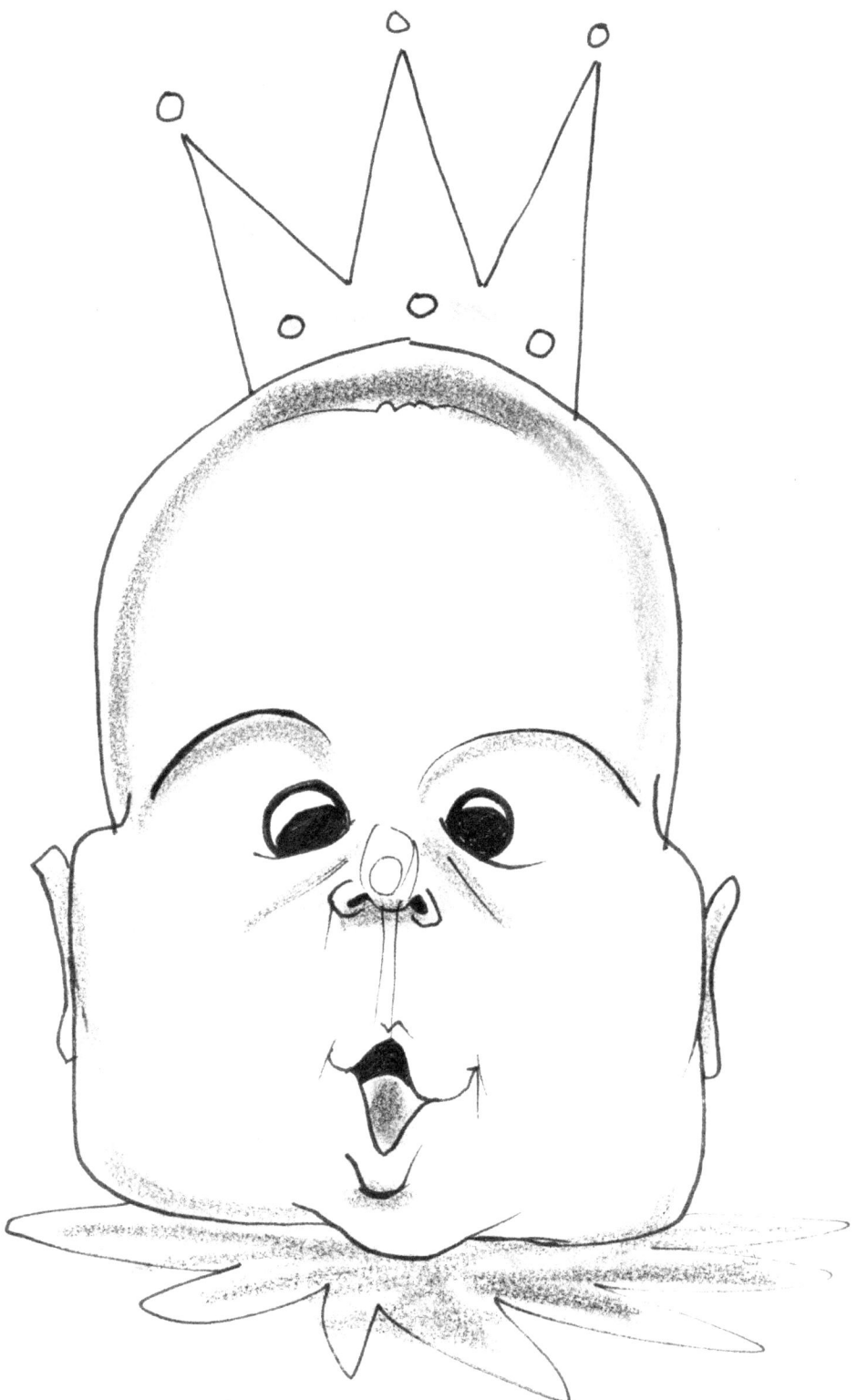

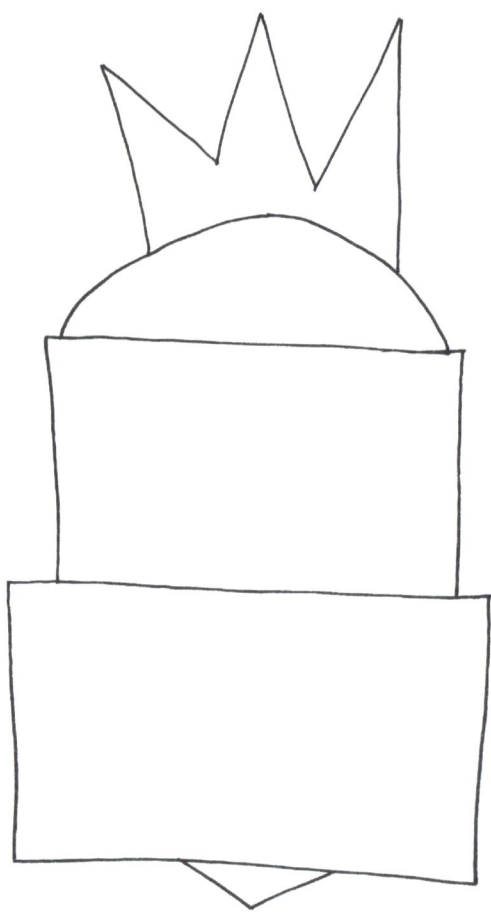

Babies can be a challenge to draw. They do not have a lot of features to exaggerate. Make the nose and chin small. Make the eyes big.

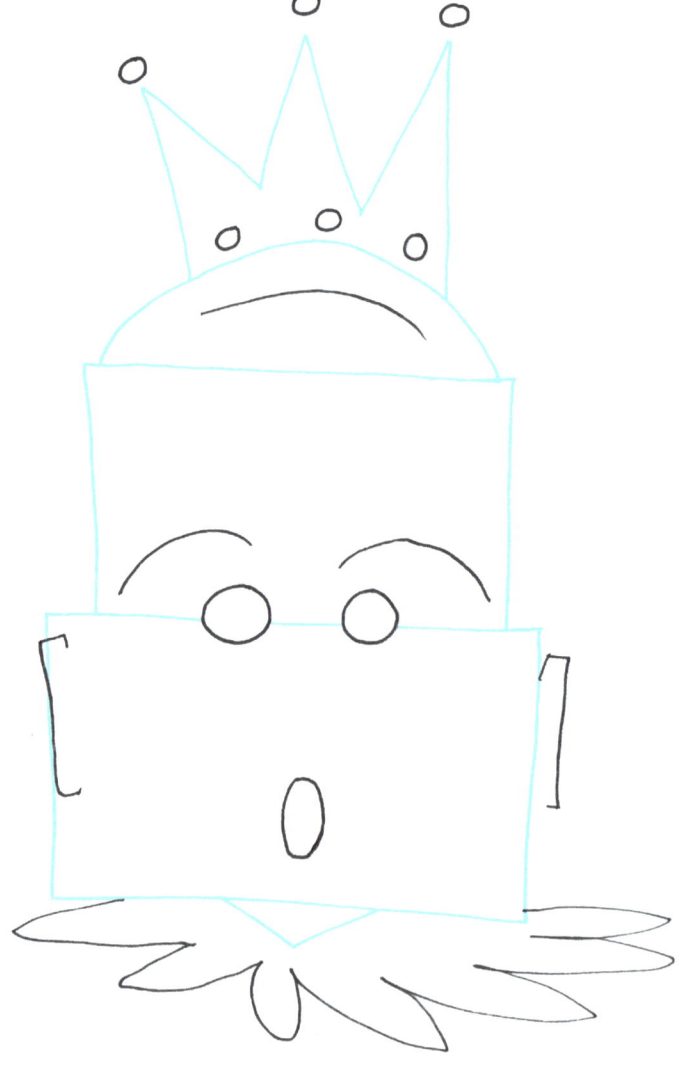

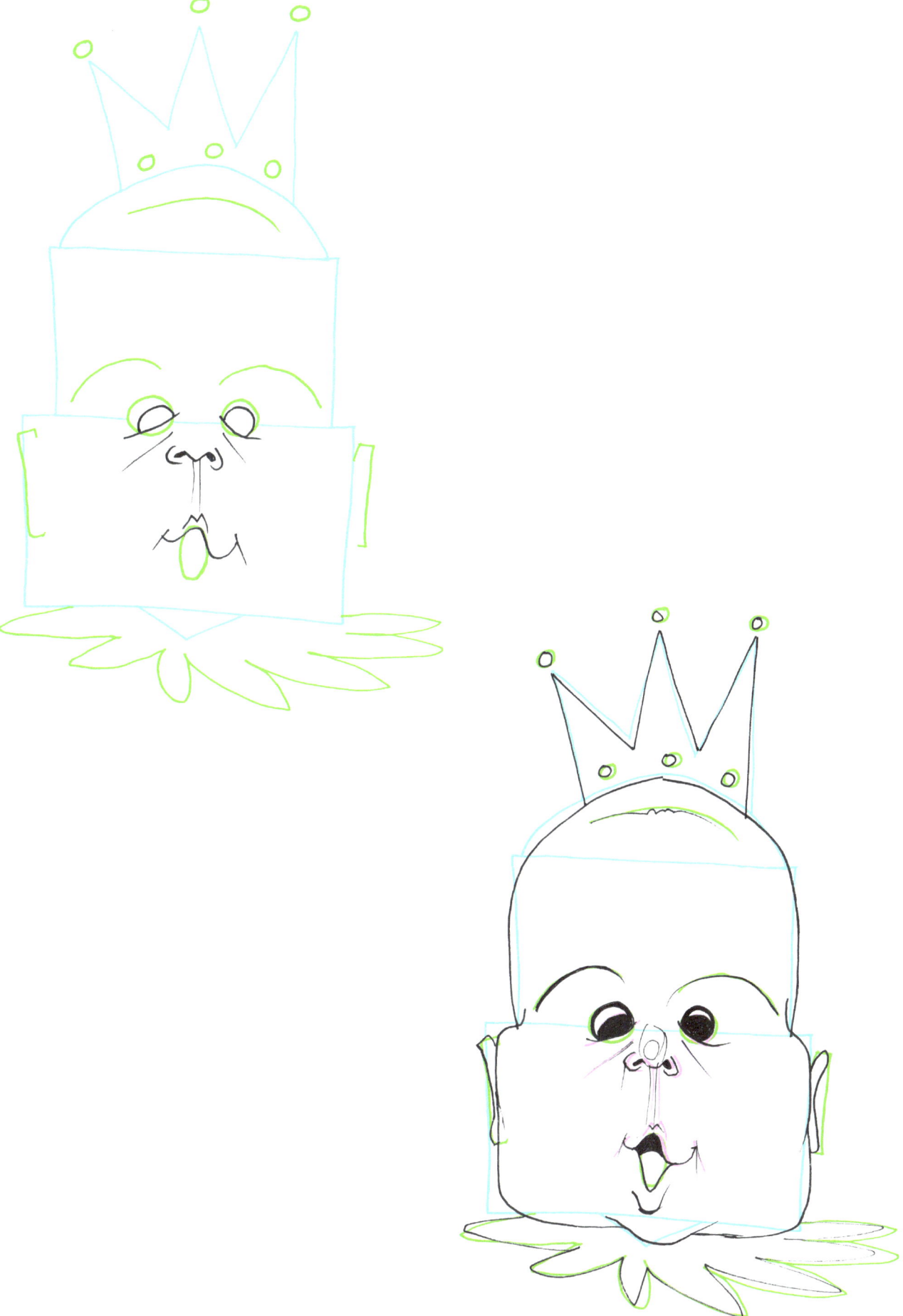

#5
Hillary Clinton

In 2013, she stepped down from the important job of United States Secretary of State. But she may have her eye on a future job: the presidency.

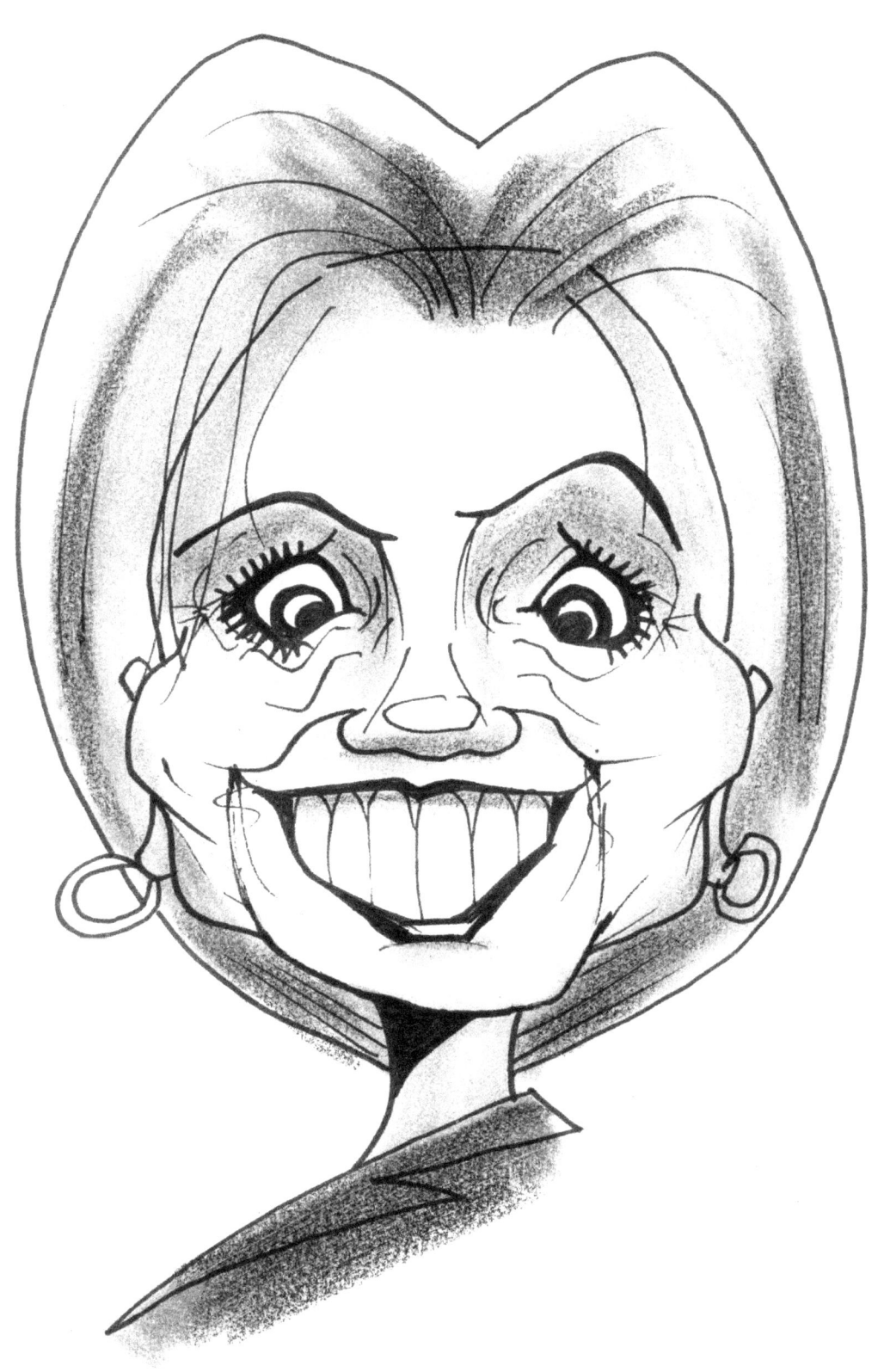

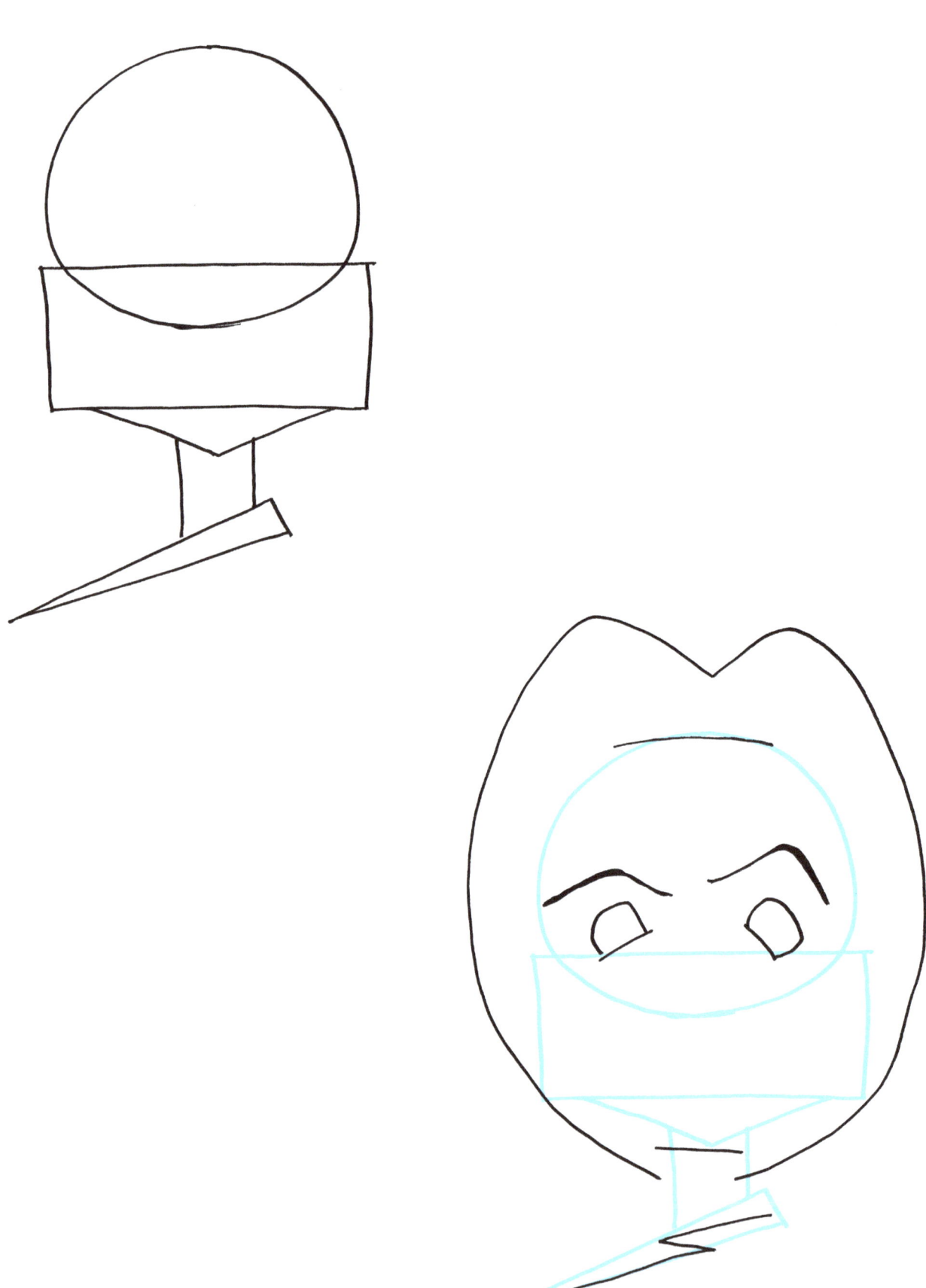

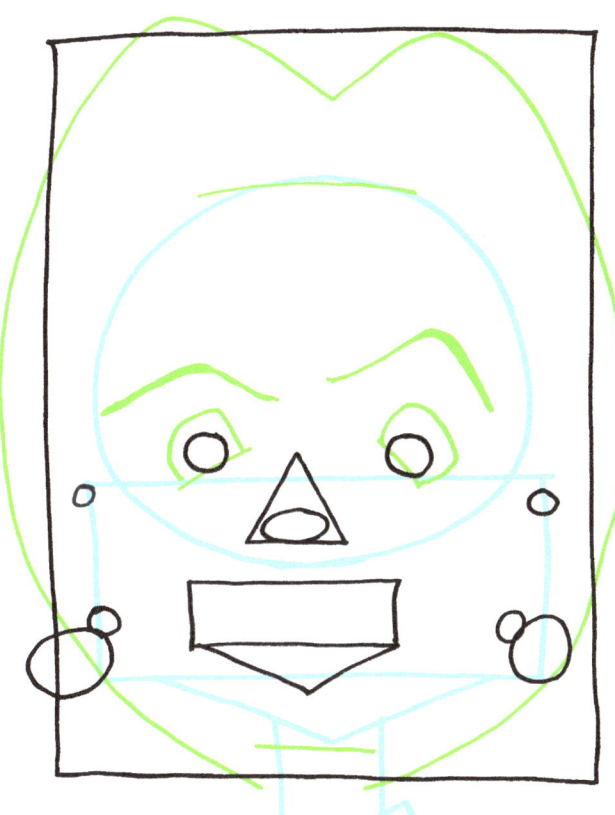

Do not give up on a drawing that does not look like the subject. Keep working. Even tiny changes can make a big difference.

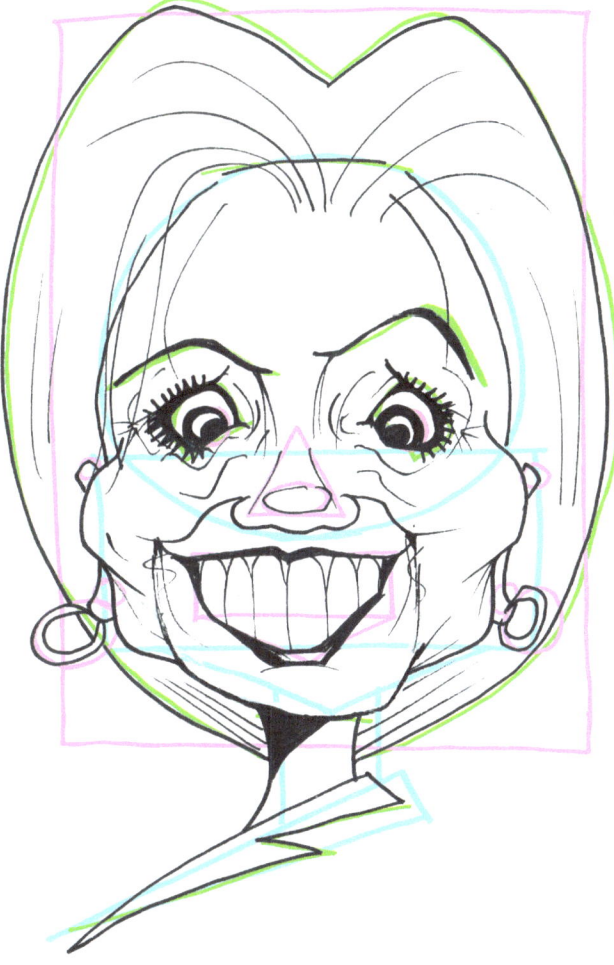

#4
Michelle Obama

The First Lady became an evangelist for good health. She urged children to eat right and exercise.

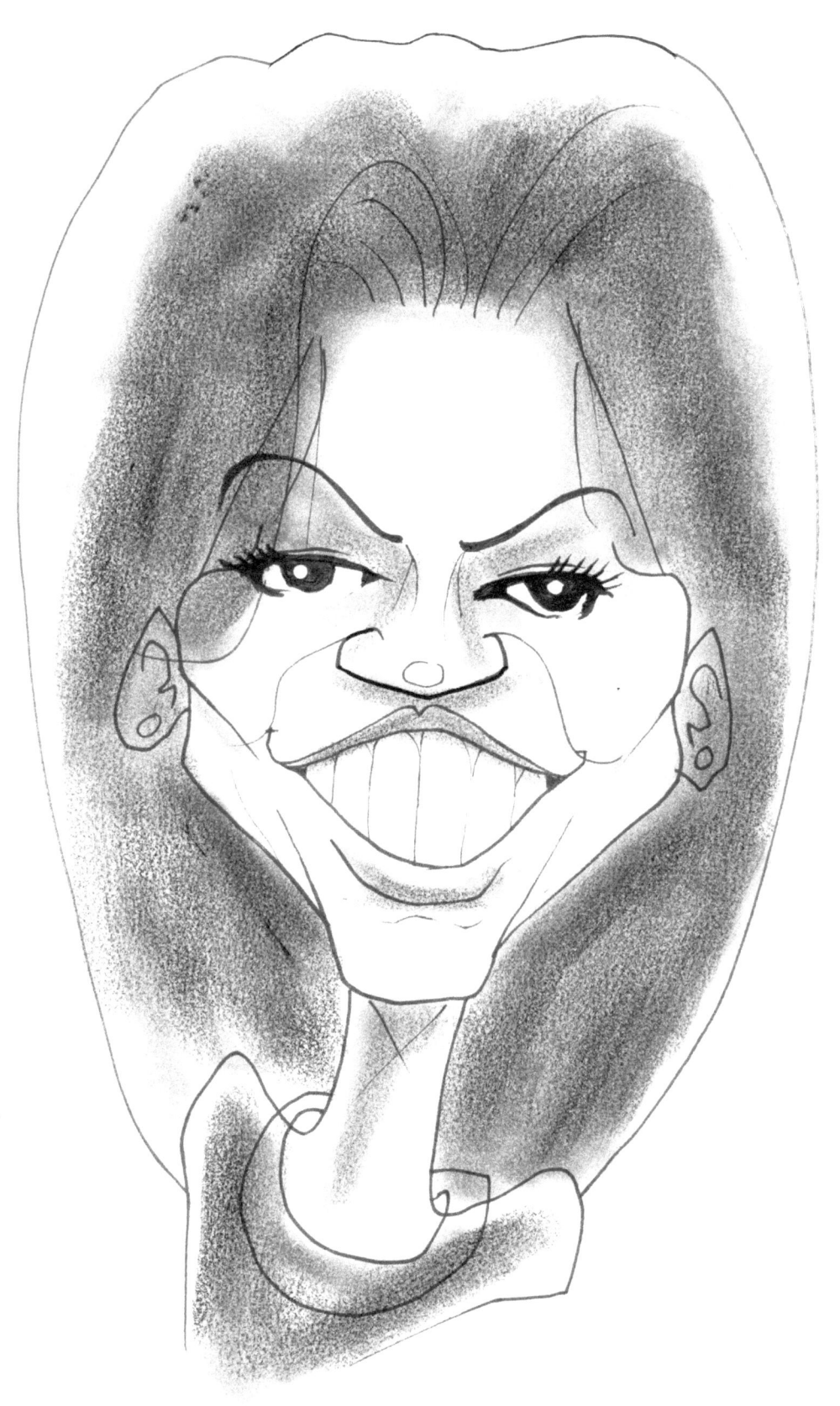

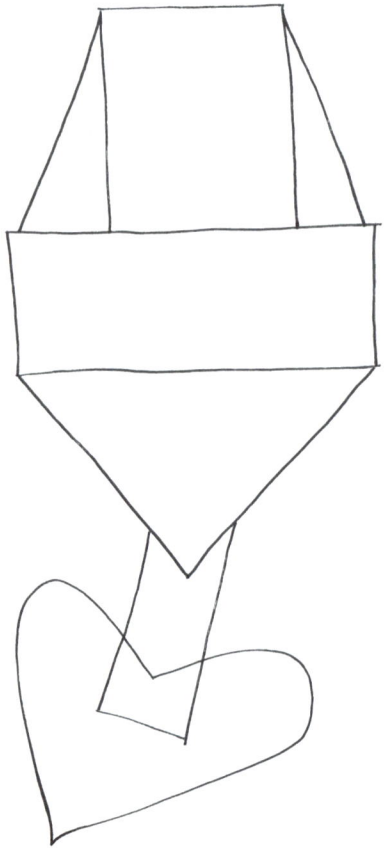

Use a light touch with your pencil as you sketch. You can always go over the lines you like best.

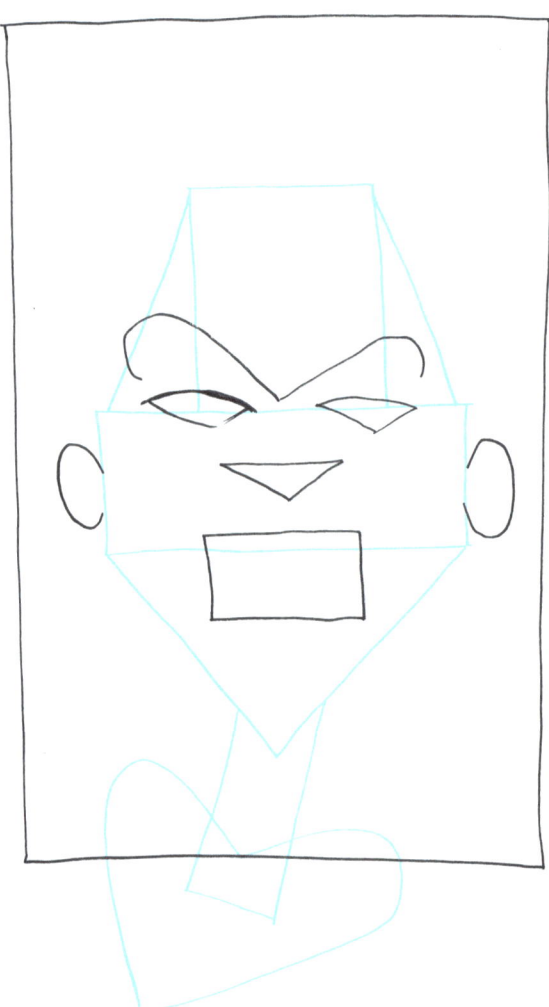

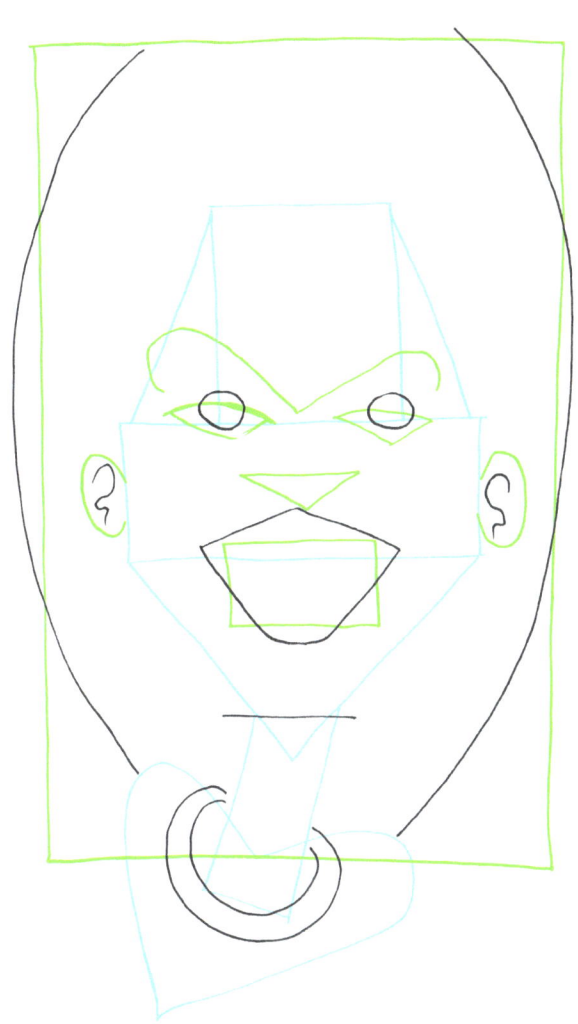
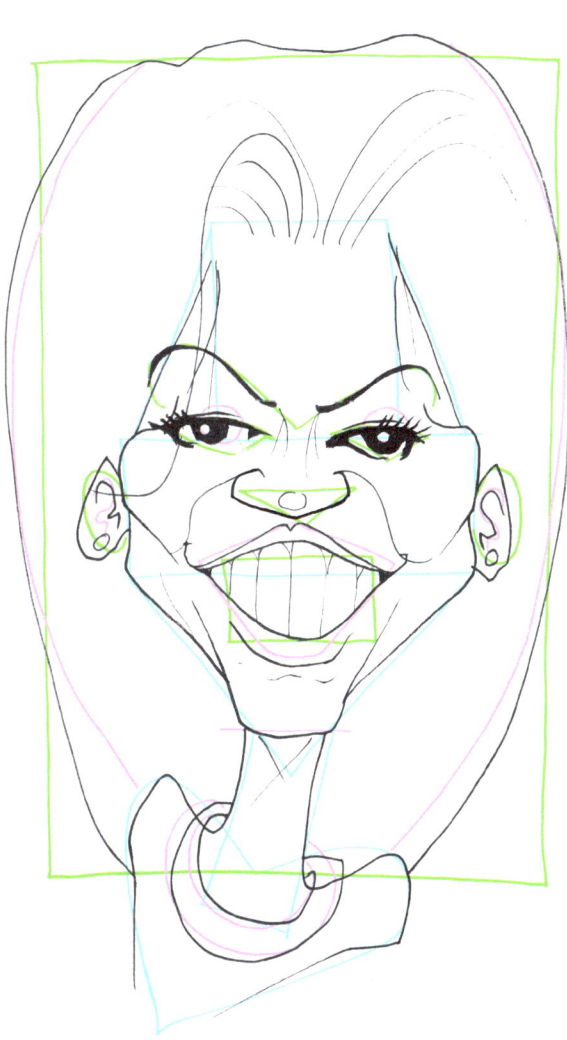

#3

Pope Francis

The first South American Pope is one of a kind. How many previous Popes could say they worked as a nightclub bouncer? His humanity fits him well, and makes it easier for the rest of us to relate to him.

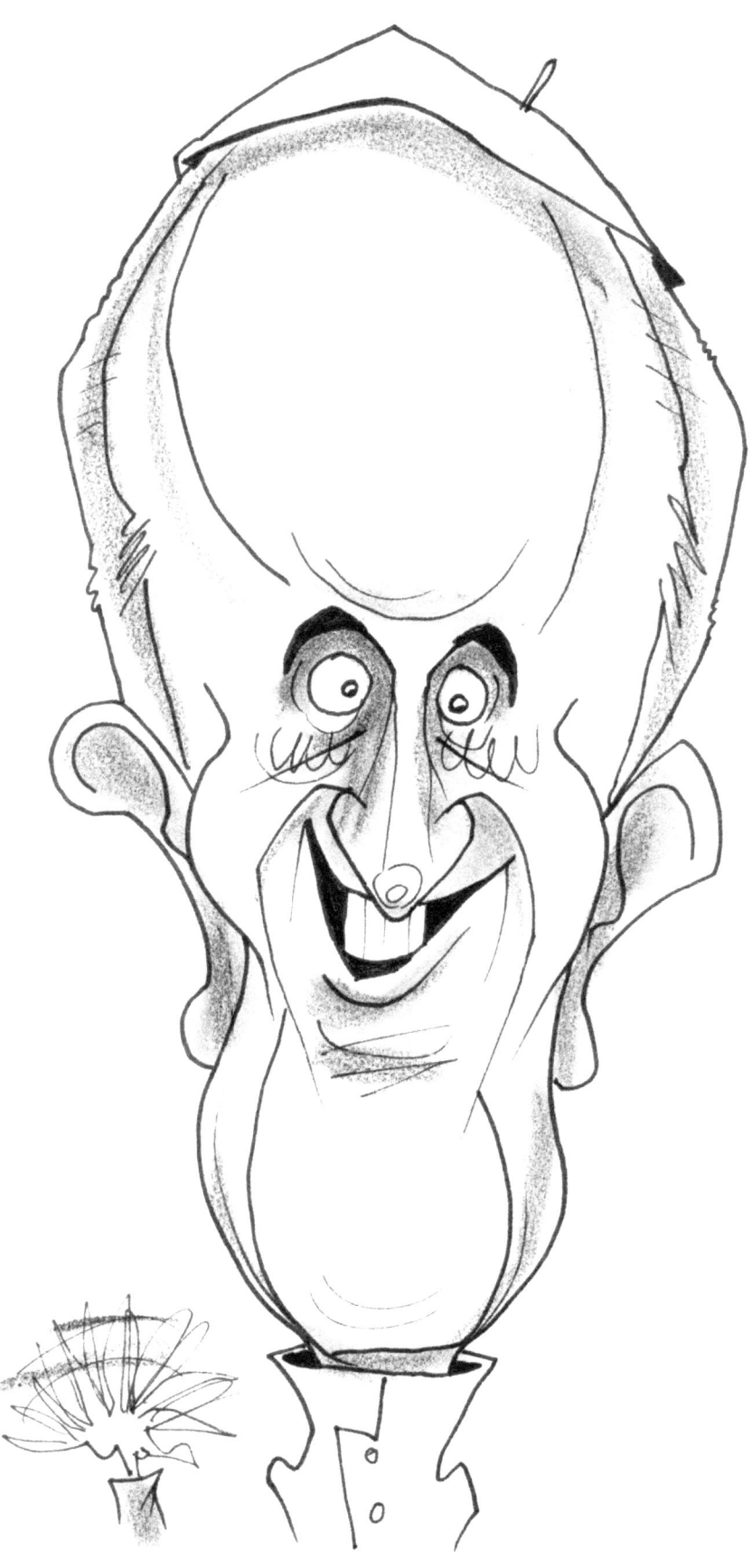

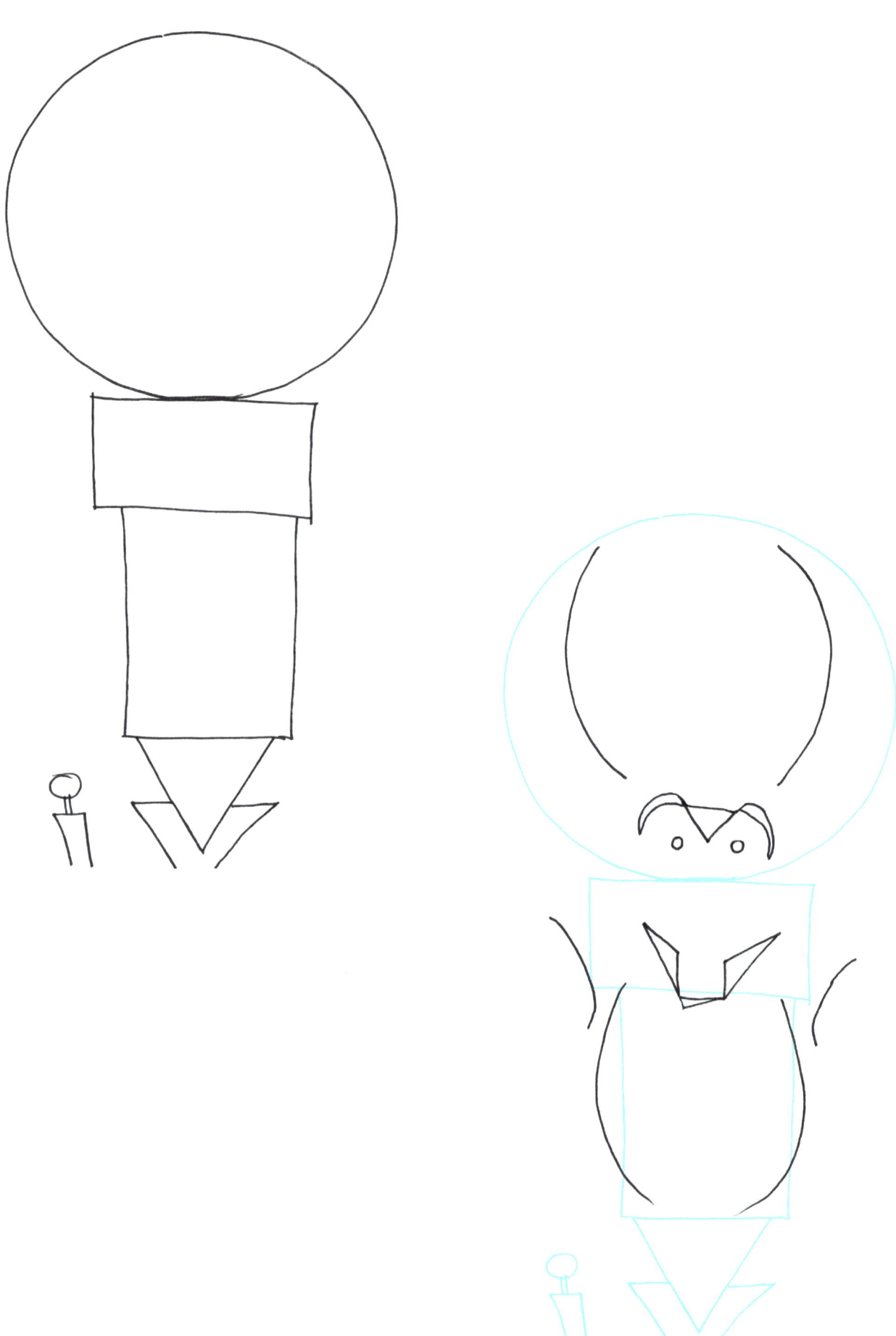

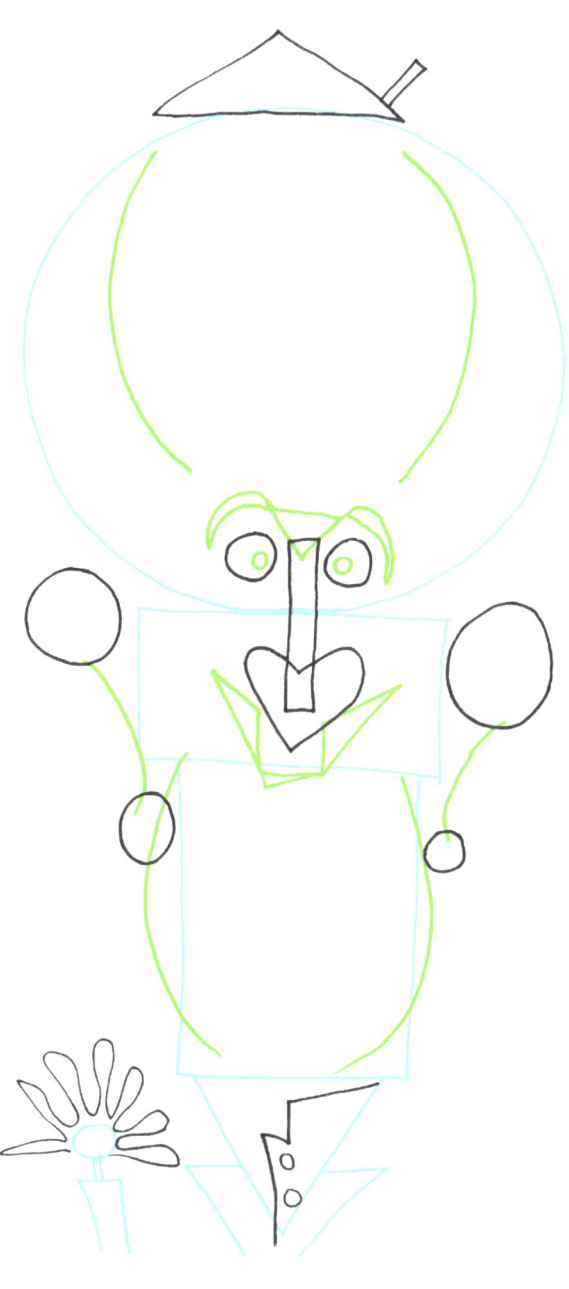

Older men make good caricature
subjects. Their features are prominent
and give artists a lot to work with.

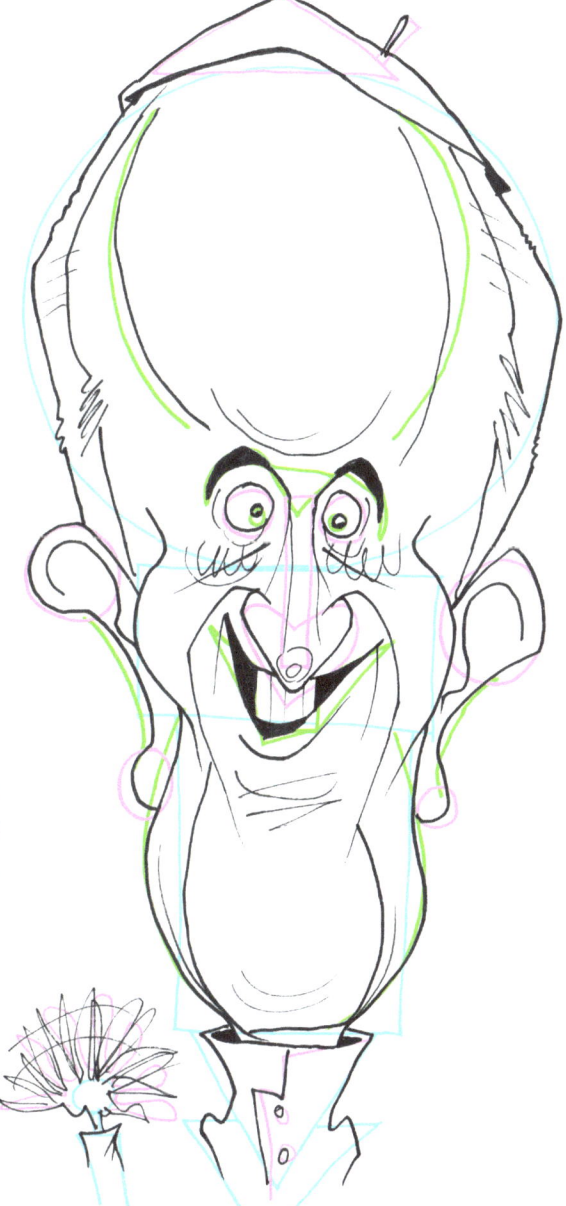

#2

Barack Obama

He will be remembered for his national health care system. Enemies of the ACA (Affordable Care Act) called it Obamacare. Friends of the plan decided they liked the name and used it, too.

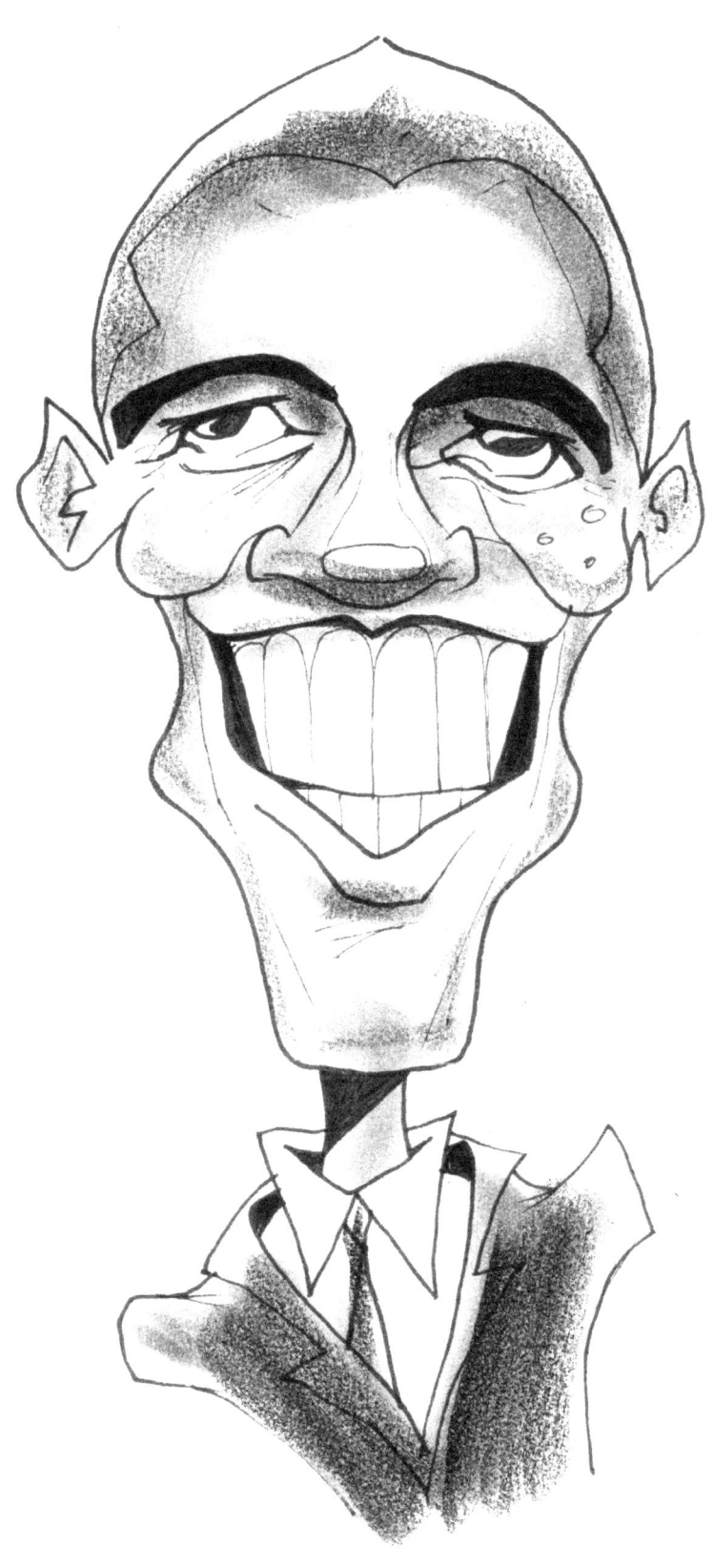

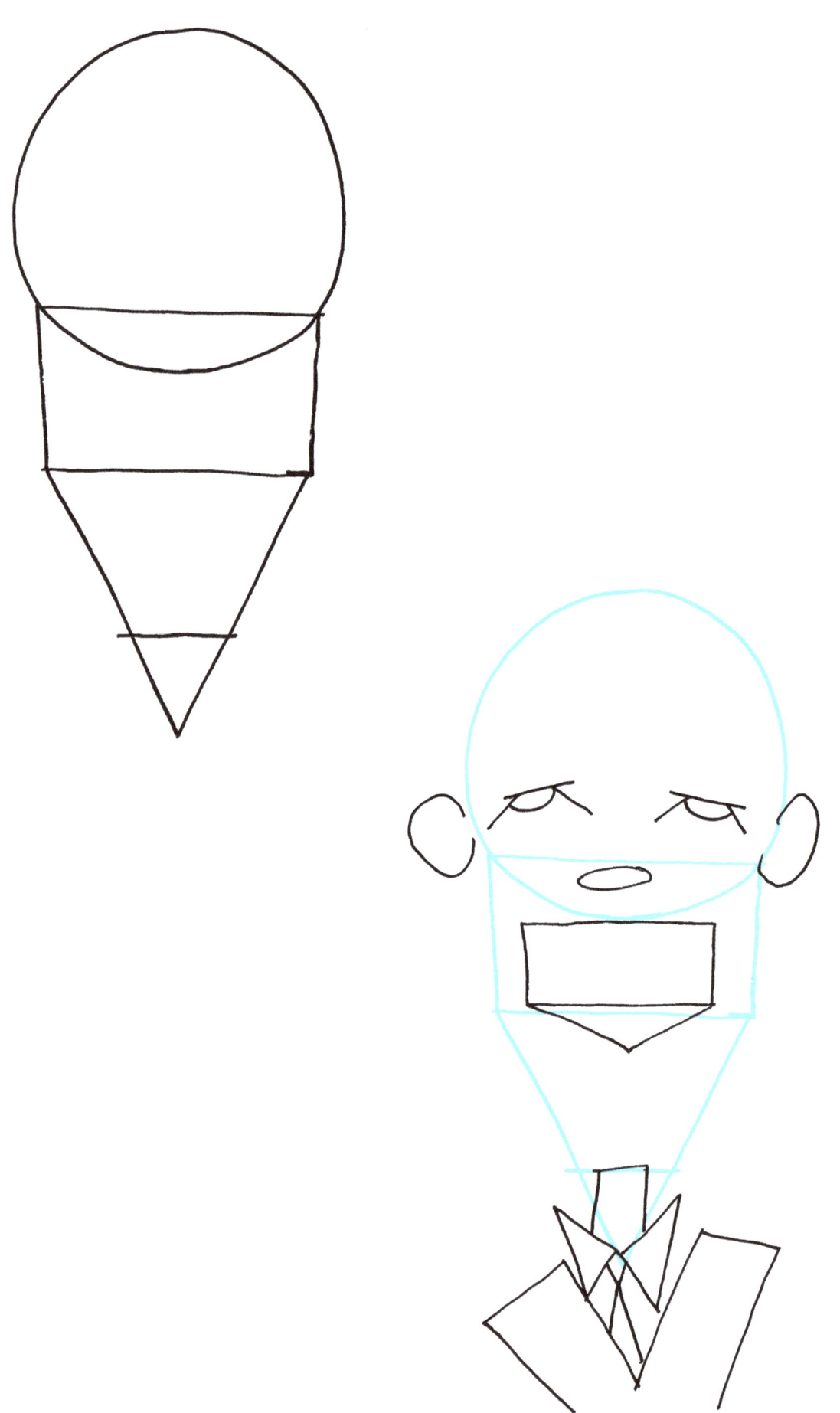

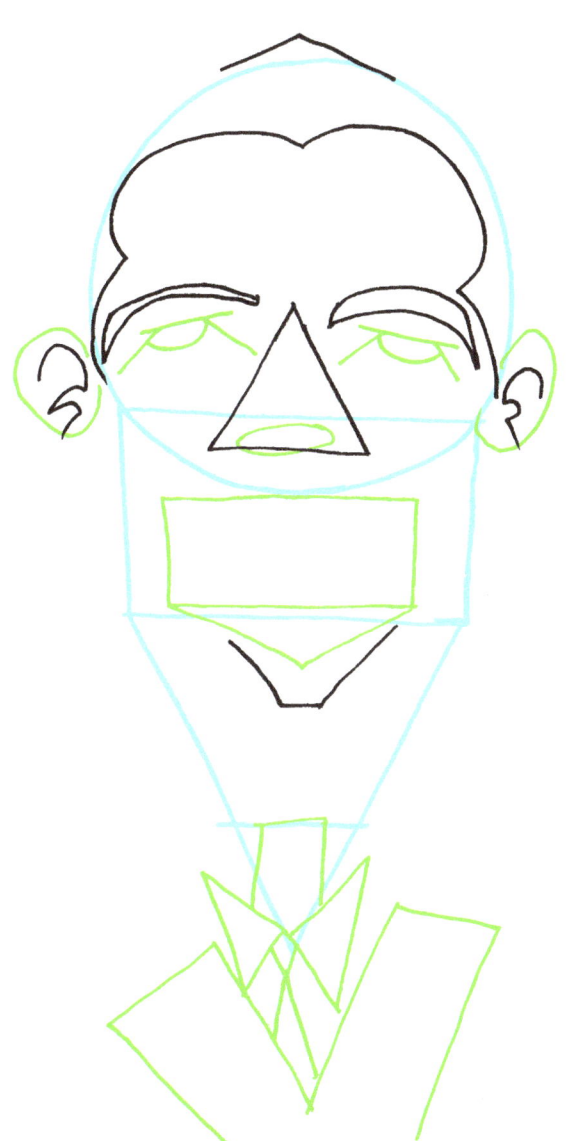

Artists usually sketch in pencil, then go over a finished drawing with pen or marker. If you do this, be sure to erase all pencil marks.

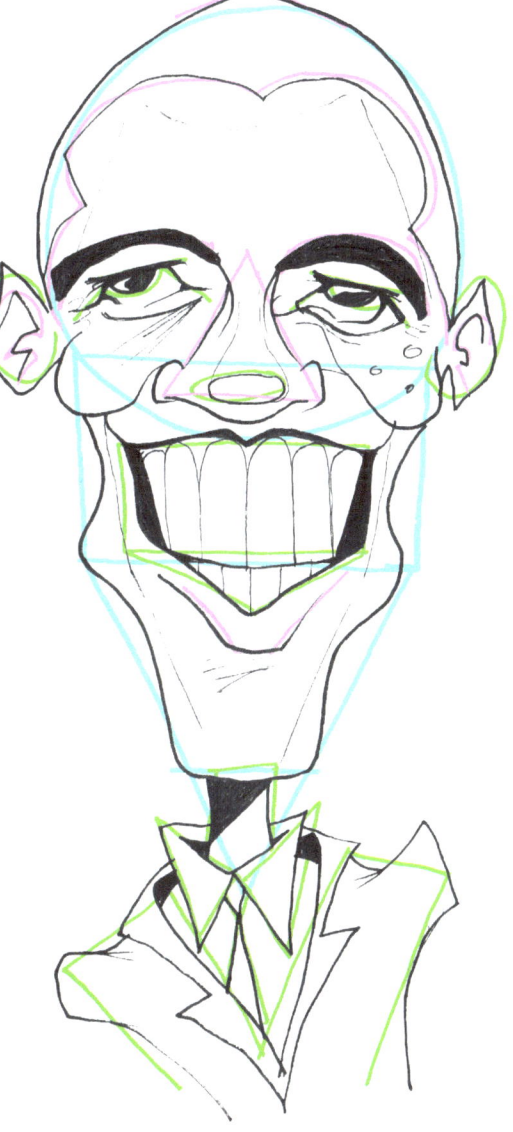

#1

Nelson Mandela

Usually a legend takes years to shape. But Nelson Mandela, the former South African president, became a legend during his lifetime. And when he died in December of 2013, Mandela immediately joined immortals like Lincoln, King and Gandhi.

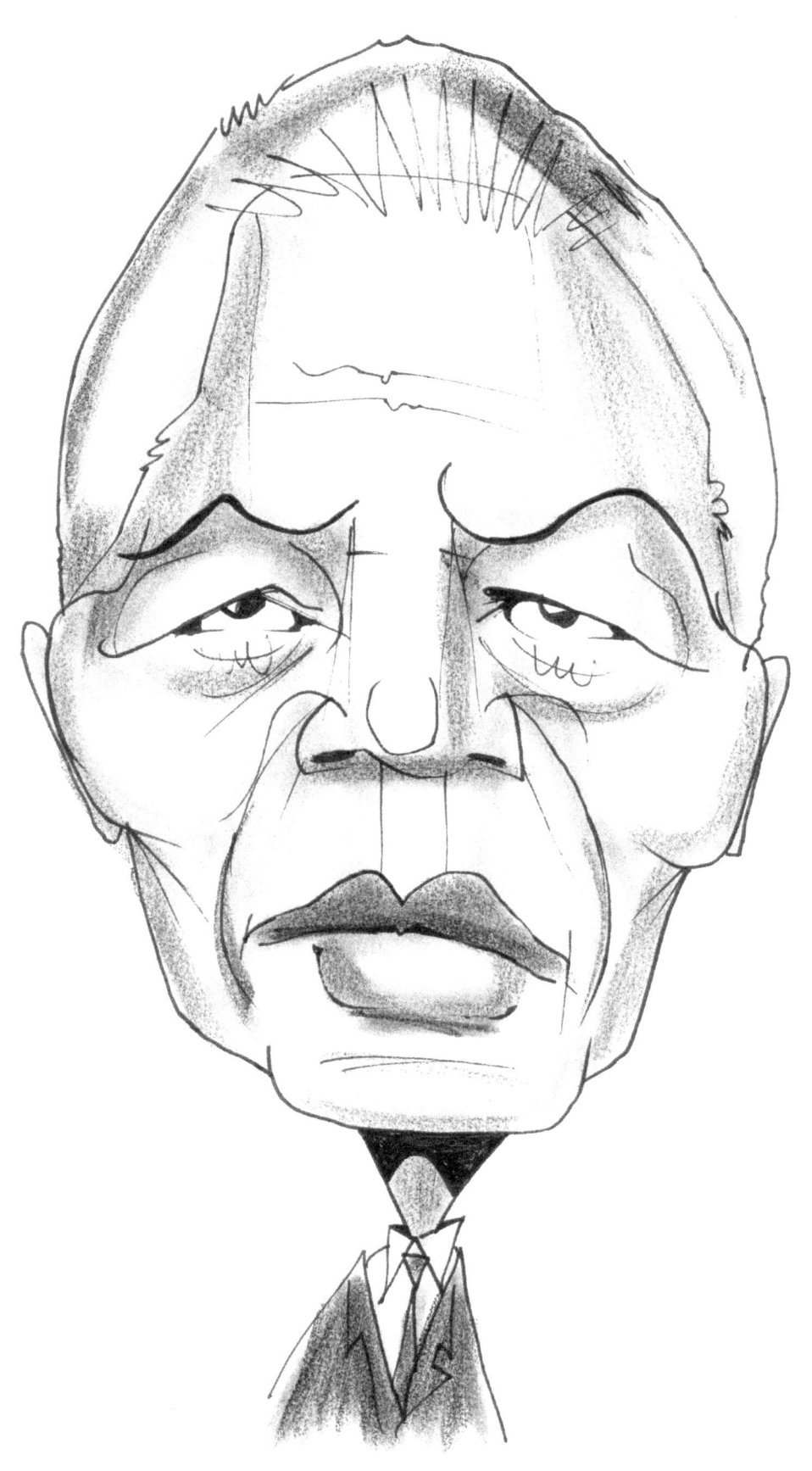

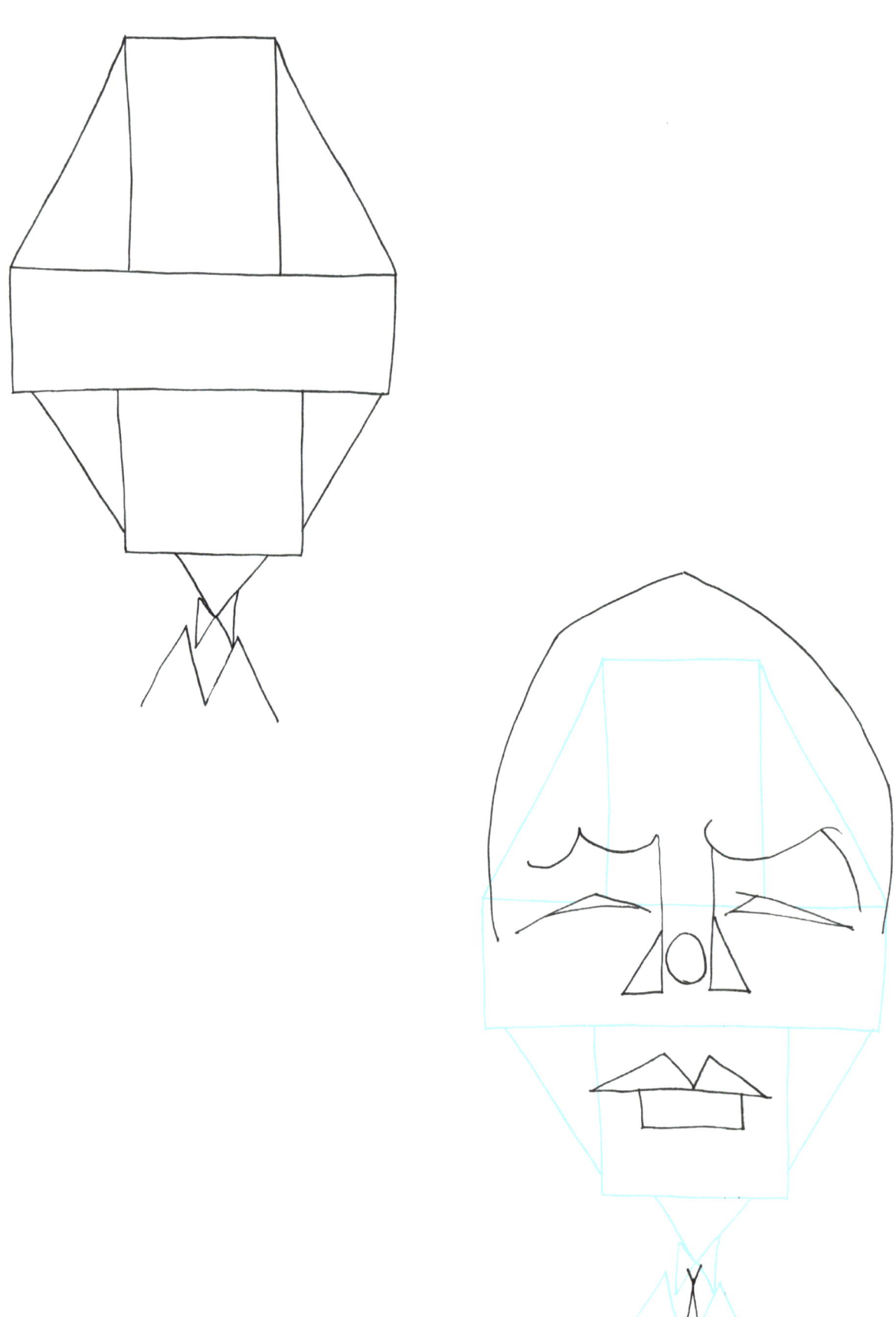

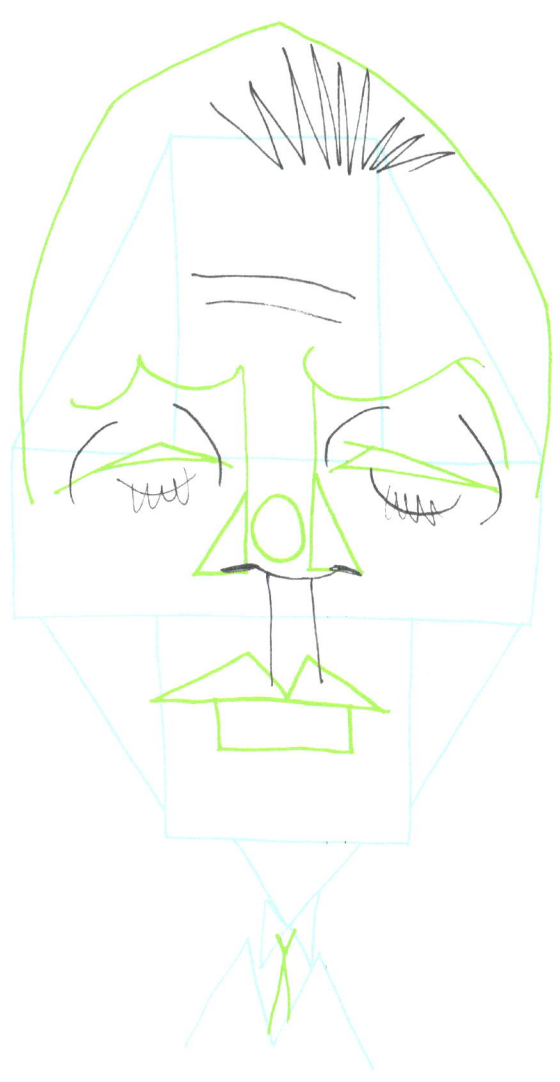

Emotion is tough to draw. But the best caricatures allow us to peek into a person's personality. Mandela led a sad life, but he was tough. And, in the end, he triumphed over unfairness.

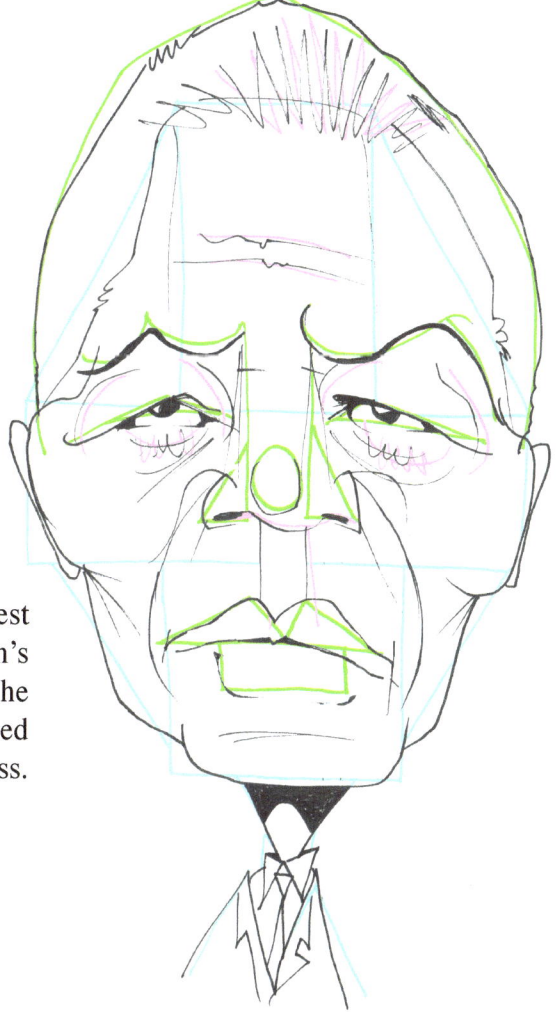

This book is at an end.

Want to draw more? Look around. There is an entire world of faces. Start with basic shapes. Add details. Work at a drawing, even if it seems hopeless at first.

And be sure to check out **www.drawingfromhistory.com** for the next book in the *Drawing From History* series.